EUROPE: THE EXCEPTIONAL CASE

SARUM THEOLOGICAL LECTURES

EUROPE:
THE EXCEPTIONAL CASE

Parameters of Faith in the Modern World

Grace Davie

DARTON · LONGMAN + TODD

For my Swedish friends
who made it all possible.

First published in 2002 by
Darton, Longman and Todd Ltd
1 Spencer Court
140–142 Wandsworth High Street
London SW18 4JJ

ISBN 0–232–52425–4

A catalogue record for this book is available from the British Library.

Designed by Sandie Boccacci
Phototypeset in 11¼/14pt Bembo
by Intype London Ltd
Printed and bound in Great Britain
by The Bath Press, Bath

CONTENTS

ACKNOWLEDGEMENTS

This book is a slightly expanded version of the Sarum Theological Lectures given in Salisbury Cathedral in April/May 2001. The lectures themselves were prepared during my tenure of the Kerstin Hesselgren Professorship in the University of Uppsala, whose facilities (not least a series of excellent libraries) provided me with the best possible conditions for research and writing. I would like to express my thanks to the many people who made this particular combination possible, my hosts at Sarum College for the kind invitation to give the lectures and the Swedish Research Council who generously funded the Chair in Uppsala.

Within this framework, other acknowledgements are more personal. I must first thank both David Catchpole and Bruce Duncan who, together with their colleagues, made me so welcome at Sarum College in May 2001. Each lecture, given in Salisbury Cathedral by kind permission of the Dean and Chapter, was a real pleasure, not least the various sociabilities that accompanied these occasions. I have also been delighted that this series of lectures, like its predecessors, should be published by Darton, Longman and Todd. I am grateful in particular to Katie Worrall and Kathy Dyke for their time and trouble with this venture.

In the University of Uppsala, my host was Anders Bäckström from the Faculty of Theology. More specifically I worked in Diakonivetenskapliga Institutet (the Uppsala Institute for Diaconal and Social Studies) which is directed by Professor Bäckström. No group of people could have made me more welcome or given me better conditions for working than those who gather at DVI. Whilst in Sweden, I was also a regular visitor to the Swedish Collegium for the Advanced Study of Social

Science, where once again I was always welcome. The theoretical aspects of my work were greatly enhanced by the discussions that I had at SCASS – with both the directors and the distinguished group of fellows who were present in the 2000–1 academic session.

Two further projects have run alongside and enhanced this one. The first has been a working group set up by the World Council of Churches to examine the changing place of religion in the modern world and its implications for the ecumenical movement. This project, convened by Julio de Santa Ana, has meant regular visits to the Ecumenical Centre at Bossey for a series of meetings in which scholars from all parts of the Christian world have been engaged. I, as a European, had everything to learn from these colleagues in discussions which were as fascinating as they were wide-ranging. Finally towards the end of the time that I spent working on this book, I was invited to join a project on Comparative Secularity directed by Peter Berger (of Boston University) and Danièle Hervieu-Léger (from the École des Hautes Études en Sciences Sociales in Paris). The notion of European exceptionalism has provided a central theme in these discussions.

I would, at this point, like to thank the various readers of the different case studies for their generosity in putting me straight in fields where I was distinctly amateur. David Martin read the chapter on Latin America, David Maxwell the chapter on Africa, and Feliciano Cariño and SungHo Kim read the relevant sections of the chapter on the Far East. The debt to David Martin is, as ever, much broader than this. Rather more generally, various parts of the argument were 'tried out' at different conferences during the 2000–1 academic session; I have been very grateful for these occasions and for the feedback that they gave me. The director and staff of the European Values Study have, finally, been invaluable both in the provision of up-to-date data and in their guidance to me about how it should be used.

My warmest thanks of all, in this project as in all others, go to my husband, who joined me in Uppsala for the second half of the year in Sweden. A time to remember!

GRACE DAVIE

Exeter, December 2001

Acknowledgements

INTRODUCTION

Above all, the Sarum Theological Lectures have offered me an opportunity to expand my thinking on the nature and development of religious activity in post-war Europe, a statement which needs to be set in the longer term. My concerns with the connections between religion and modernity date from the mid 1980s. The canvas on which I have worked has, however, steadily widened: from an initial engagement with faith in the inner cities of modern Britain (Ahern and Davie 1987), through a more general consideration of the religious life of Britain in the post-war period (Davie 1994), to a concern with the patterns of religion in modern Europe (Davie 2000a). Each book has led to the next: patterns of working-class belief, common since the nineteenth century, have become the norm in Britain as a whole; the same patterns, unchurched and residually Christian religion, are widespread, if not universal, in Western Europe at the start of the twenty-first century.

The next step is to place Europe itself within a global context, but at this point the narrative takes a rather different turn. It is simply not the case that the patterns of religious activity discovered in Western Europe are those of the modern world more generally. Indeed, if anything, the reverse is true. In terms of the parameters of faith of the modern world, the European case is beginning to look increasingly like an exception – a statement that many Europeans find hard to accept in that it flies in the face not only of their own experience, but of deeply embedded assumptions. Europeans are prone to believe that what they do today everyone else will do tomorrow. Or in terms of the subject matter of this series of lectures, Europeans are convinced that the relatively strong empirical connections between modernisation and secularisation that can be observed in Europe's historical evolution will necessarily be repeated elsewhere. Hence their conviction that as the world modernises, it will necessarily secularise.

Quite simply, it hasn't. And one look at the empirical evidence taken from almost every other global region suggests that it won't in the foreseeable future. Even if we restrict the discussion to Christendom, an entirely different combination of factors obtains in, for example, the United States, in Latin America, in sub-Saharan Africa and in a significant number of Eastern societies, notably the Philippines or South Korea. In these parts of the world, there is scant evidence for secularisation, despite in many cases (if not all) convincing indicators of modernisation – most notably in the United States (the most developed society in the world). Add to this already extensive list the parts of the world dominated by other world faiths – the hugely varied Islamic nations (themselves at very different stages of development), the competing religious traditions of the Middle East, the Sikhs and Hindus of the Indian sub-continent and the great diversity of Eastern religions – and Peter Berger's claim that the greater part of the world (both developed and developing) is 'as furiously religious as ever' (Berger 1992) seems well justified.

Where, though, does this leave the question of European as opposed to other forms of religion? They must be seen, surely, as one strand among many which make up what it means to be European. European religion is not a model for export; it is something distinct, peculiar to the European corner of the world and needs to be understood in these terms. Davie (2000a) explores this theme in some detail, examining Europe from the inside (see Chapter One). Two further tasks follow on: that is (a) to look again at those parts of the world which manifest very different patterns of religious activity, asking in each case what are the attributes displayed which are *not* present in Europe (and why) and (b) to open up the conceptual implications of these findings. These tasks provide the principal aims of this book.

The work will be structured as follows. Chapter One will set out the parameters of faith in modern Europe, noting both the classic and more innovative explanations for these findings. Chapters Two to Five will develop a set of contrasting case studies, all of them drawn from Christendom, but from very different global regions: the United States, Latin America, sub-Saharan Africa and (selectively) the Far East. Each will be used to illustrate a particular point of difference with the European case, asking very precisely what is present in these examples but not in Europe. A final chapter will address the theoretical questions that must follow, not least the implications of these findings for Europe itself. Looked at from the outside we begin to see Europe in a new light and to think differently about the possible futures for religion in this part of the world. It is at least plausible that Europeans are not so much less religious than populations in other parts of the world, but differently so. Such a statement has practical as well as theoretical implications for the churches.

Two further preliminaries are necessary in this introduction. The first is a matter of definition. When speaking of Europe, I will in fact be referring to Western Europe in the sense of Western Christianity. I will not be including the Orthodox parts of Europe, nor the complex marchlands that lie between the two halves of the continent. The reason is a practical one: it is too soon to say whether the Eastern European case will follow the Western one in terms of its religious trajectory or whether a substantially new variant or variants will emerge. It is, therefore, the comparisons with the relatively stable West European situation that form the focus of the following chapters.

The second preliminary concerns my own competence. In no way do I consider myself a specialist on patterns of religion in the modern world outside Europe. I have visited the United States many times and on one occasion moved rather tentatively across the border into Mexico. Beyond this, however, I have relied entirely on secondary sources and conversations with scholars who specialise in the various fields. I am deeply grateful to the many who have given me their time and their advice in order to make the chapters that follow as accurate and as well informed as possible, but I alone am responsible for the errors that remain. It is important to remember finally that none of these chapters constitutes a comprehensive account of the religious situation in that place. They are highly selective, they are different from each other and each has been written with the intention of illustrating a particular point (or points) of contrast with Europe. There is, however, an underlying theme: that is to expose the 'boundedness' of both the European case itself and the sociological theories that have arisen from this. Such limitations are revealed bit by bit in the course of the case studies; they are brought together in the more theoretical account offered in the final chapter.

SETTING THE SCENE:
THE PARAMETERS OF FAITH
IN MODERN EUROPE

The aim of this chapter is to sharpen the reader's awareness of a situation that is so familiar that it tends to be taken for granted. We need to look critically at the parameters of faith in our own corner of the world before we can (a) compare these with other global regions and (b) make sense of the long-term future. In order to do this, the initial part of the chapter will be divided into three sections: the first will announce a theme; the second will present the principal variations on the theme that exist in different parts of Europe; and the third will introduce both the classic and more recent theoretical explanations for these findings. The fourth and final section will introduce the case studies that are to follow, with some justification for their selection and for this way of working. With the exception of a few paragraphs, the discussion in the initial sections will deal with the mainstream traditions (Europe's historic churches), rather than the important religious minorities that form part of most European societies. Despite the growing significance of faiths other than Christian in the European context, it is the dominant trends that need highlighting in the first instance.

For a British audience or readership, a preliminary point is crucial: the parameters of faith in modern Britain are very similar to our European partners. Despite marked differences in language, in denomination (there are, for example, very few Anglicans or Methodists in continental Europe), and in the very diverse legal arrangements between Church and State, there is a common thread which binds together almost all European societies in terms of their religious behaviour.

How, then, can these patterns of religious activity be discerned? There are two ways of doing this: one historical and the second empirical. The historical perspective stresses the formative factors or themes that come together in the creation and re-creation of the unity that we call Europe: these are Judaeo-Christian monotheism, Greek rationalism and Roman organisation (O'Connell 1991). These factors shift and evolve over time, but their combinations can be seen forming and re-forming a way of life that we have come to recognise as European. The religious strand within such combinations is self-evident, but so too are the *relationships* between political and religious power that have dominated so much of European history. These shared legacies go back as far as Constantine; they are deeply embedded in the European psyche, though the particular forms that they have taken in later centuries vary very considerably (a point to which we shall return). Some form of church/state connection is, however, historically present in every European society, quite apart from the crucial, if not always harmonious, relationships between pope and emperor in the centuries preceding the emergence of the nation state as the dominant form of political organisation in this part of the world.

Nor can such connections be altered at will in terms of their long-term effects. It is, of course, possible, for individual European societies to disconnect the links between Church and

State at a particular and frequently pivotal point in their history. Many societies already have (some peaceably, some after maximum contention), and no doubt others will – including, quite possibly, our own. The historical legacy is, however, harder to eradicate, not least the cultural assumptions that go with these long-term associations. This, for example, will be one of the sharpest contrasts between Europe and the United States that will emerge in the following chapter. The point to be made in this one is that constitutional connections between Church and State are part of Europe's history, whether they are retained or rejected, applauded or critiqued. Such is not necessarily the case elsewhere.[1]

A second source of material concerns empirical data – that is the findings of increasing numbers of statistical enquiries concerning the state of faith both in Europe as a whole and in its constituent nations. One example can be taken as representative: the European Values Study.[2] It, like so many others of its kind,[3] uses sophisticated social science methodology (including careful sampling techniques) to establish patterns and connections between different kinds of variables – in this case to map social and moral values across Europe, relating these to a range of economic and social indicators. It has generated very considerable data and will continue to do so. Any serious commentator on the religious situation in modern Europe must pay close, but at the same time critical, attention to its findings.

The EVS is concerned with two underlying themes: the first concerns the substance of contemporary European values and asks, in particular, to what extent they are homogeneous; the second takes a more dynamic approach, asking to what extent such values are changing. Both themes inevitably involve a religious element, either directly or indirectly. The first of these themes (the substance and the similarity of European value systems) is widely accepted. The empirical data from the EVS confirm the notion that the value systems of modern Europe (including Britain, whatever our misgivings in this respect) have a considerable amount in common, a fact most easily explained by a shared religious heritage. No one disputes that the Judaeo-Christian tradition – massively present in all parts of Europe – was a crucial factor in the formation of European values, albeit in connection with a great many other variables.

As soon as the idea of value change is engaged, however, the debate becomes both complex and at times contentious. On the one hand, the authority of both the institutional churches and the creeds that underpin them is systematically decreasing as the decades pass. No one seriously doubts this. On the other, it is difficult to discern what, if anything, is emerging to replace these social and cultural forms. As the EVS writers have themselves pointed out (Barker *et al.*, 1992: 7), the Church has indeed lost its role as the keystone in the arch of European culture, but no identifiable institution is emerging to take its place. Hence a whole series of questions with respect to the future of European religion and its continued influence on the value system. It is these questions that form the substance of the secularisation debate; they and some possible answers will be developed through the course of this chapter. In terms of the book as a whole, however, a further point immediately presents itself: is this situation unique to this part of the world (and if so why) or can it be found elsewhere? Herein lies the *fil conducteur* of the Sarum Theological Lectures.

The first task, however, is to indicate the principal findings of the 1981, 1990 and 1999 EVS surveys for a variety of religious indicators.[4] Here the material draws very directly on my previous work (especially Davie 2000a: 5–23), to which the reader is directed for a fuller discussion. The central point to grasp, however, lies in the multiplicity of variables that need to be taken into account in any assessment of the religious situation of modern Europe. Five of these can be found within the EVS data: they are denominational allegiance, reported church attendance, attitudes towards the Church, indicators of religious belief and some measurement of subjective religious disposition.

Such data permit, moreover, considerable flexibility, the more so given modern techniques of data analysis: the variables can be correlated both with each other and with a wide range of socio-demographic data. Hence the complexity of the emergent patterns and the need to bear in mind more than one dimension within an individual's (or indeed a nation's) religious life in coming to any conclusions.

What emerges in practice, however, is the situation that I have described elsewhere as 'believing without belonging' (Davie 1994) – a phrase that has become popular in pastoral as well as academic circles, and which undoubtedly captures the clustering of two types of variable: on the one hand, those concerned with feelings, experience and the more numinous religious beliefs; on the other, those which measure religious orthodoxy, ritual participation and institutional attachment. A second observation follows from this. It is only the latter (i.e. the more orthodox indicators of religious attachment) which display an undeniable degree of secularisation throughout Western Europe. In contrast, the former (the less institutional indicators) demonstrate considerable persistence (see below). The essentials of this contrasting information are presented in Tables 1.1 and 1.2, reproduced from the EVG data. These tables can be used in two ways: either to indicate the overall picture of the continent or to exemplify some of the marked national differences that can be found within Europe as a whole. In this section the emphasis will lie on the former; the differences form the background to the next.

It is clear, first of all, that the data are complex. With this in mind, I am hesitant about the unqualified use of the term secularisation even in the European context. Indeed it seems to me considerably more accurate to suggest that West Europeans remain, by and large, unchurched populations rather than simply secular. For a marked falling-off in religious attendance (especially in the Protestant North) has not resulted, yet, in a parallel abdication of religious belief – in a broad definition of

Table 1.1 Frequency of church attendance in West Europe 1999/2000 (some examples) %

	Once a week	Once a month	Special occasions	Never
European average	20.5	10.8	38.8	29.5
CATHOLIC COUNTRIES				
Belgium	19.0	9.0	25.3	46.6
France	7.6	4.3	27.8	60.4
Ireland	56.9	10.5	22.8	9.7
Italy	40.5	13.1	32.5	13.9
Portugal	36.4	14.9	33.5	15.2
Spain	25.5	10.5	32.5	31.5
MIXED COUNTRIES				
Great Britain	14.4	4.5	25.3	55.8
Germany	13.6	16.5	41.2	28.8
Netherlands	14.5	11.2	28.1	46.1
Northern Ireland	48.5	14.9	16.9	19.8
LUTHERAN COUNTRIES				
Denmark	2.7	9.2	45.4	42.7
Finland	5.3	8.8	59.8	26.2
Iceland	3.2	8.8	55.6	32.3
Sweden	3.8	5.5	90.5	0.2
ORTHODOX COUNTRIES				
Greece	22.3	20.9	53.9	2.8

Data supplied by the European Values Study, University of Tilburg

Europe: The Exceptional Case

Table 1.2 Extent of religious belief in West Europe 1999/2000 (some examples) %

Belief in:	God	Life after death	Heaven	Hell	Sin
European average	77.4	53.3	46.3	33.9	62.1
CATHOLIC COUNTRIES					
Belgium	71.4	45.6	33.5	19.3	44.1
France	61.5	44.7	31.2	19.6	39.8
Ireland	95.5	79.2	85.3	53.4	85.7
Italy	93.5	72.8	58.7	49.0	73.2
Portugal	96.4	47.3	60.0	37.8	71.2
Spain	86.7	49.9	50.8	32.9	51.2
MIXED COUNTRIES					
Great Britain	71.6	58.3	55.8	35.3	66.9
Germany	67.8	38.8	30.9	20.1	41.3
Netherlands	61.1	50.1	37.4	13.8	39.7
Northern Ireland	93.2	75.1	86.6	73.9	90.4
LUTHERAN COUNTRIES					
Denmark	68.9	38.3	18.4	9.5	20.6
Finland	82.5	56.7	61.4	31.4	67.1
Iceland	84.4	78.2	58.7	17.5	64.3
Sweden	53.4	46.0	31.2	9.4	25.7
ORTHODOX COUNTRIES					
Greece	93.8	59.2	59.1	52.6	83.3

Data supplied by European Values Study, University of Tilburg

the term. In short, many Europeans have ceased to connect with their religious institutions in any active sense, but they have not abandoned, so far, either their deep-seated religious aspirations or (in many cases) a latent sense of belonging.

This mismatch between belief and practice raises, in fact, one of the crucial questions of the EVG material. It is, moreover, a topic which divides the commentators (themselves from a variety of disciplines), who have made use of these data. On the one hand, there are those who assume that belief will follow practice downwards, but at a slower rate. In other words, the two variables are directly related and will move in the same direction, albeit at different speeds. On the other, there are commentators (including myself) who consider belief a more independent variable. An evident fall in both religious practice and *strictly Christian* beliefs in the post-war period does not lead either to a parallel loss in religious sensitivity (indeed the reverse is often true as individuals sense a greater freedom to experiment), or to the widespread adoption of secular alternatives (here the point should be made even more emphatically). Hence a rather different conclusion: religious belief is *inversely* rather than *directly* related to belonging. In other words, as the institutional disciplines decline, belief not only persists, but becomes increasingly personal, detached and heterogeneous and particularly among young people. The data from the most recent European Values Study (1999/2000) strongly reinforce this point.[5]

In the meantime, it is important to note a number of other patterns that emerge from the EVG data. Significant here are the correlations that obtain between religious indices and a range of socio-economic variables, all of which confirm the existence of socio-religious patterning across national boundaries. The most striking of these concern the correlations with both gender and age throughout West Europe. The disproportionate presence of women in almost every kind of religious activity (both belief and practice) can in fact be found throughout the Christian West, a point to which we shall return in some detail with respect to the Latin American material. The correlation with age, in contrast, prompts one of the most searching questions of the European Values Study: is West Europe experiencing a permanent generational shift with respect to religious behaviour, rather than a manifestation of the normal life-cycle? The EVG findings indicate that this might be so. The precise direction of such changes remains extremely difficult to predict, however – the more so given the conclusions of the previous paragraph.

There are, finally, shifts occurring throughout Western Europe in terms of the changing nature of the religious population. Such data cannot be found in the EVG, or indeed in any comparable survey, given that the sample sizes for each country are too small to provide any meaningful information about religious minorities. They are, none the less, of crucial importance for our understanding of Europe's religious environment. Despite the necessary emphasis in this chapter on the historic churches, it would, I think, be unwise to ignore the minorities completely.

The first of these, the Jews, has been present in Europe for centuries, though not continuously so, a fact in itself indicative of the tragedies of European history, both more and less recent. It also demonstrates the inapplicability of the term Judaeo-Christian to much of Europe's past. The term (more related to American political correctness than historical accuracy) should be used with considerable caution. Estimates of numbers are always difficult, but there are, at present, around one million Jews in West Europe, the largest communities being the French (500,000–600,000) and the British (300,000). French Judaism has been transformed in the post-war period by the immigration of considerable numbers of Sephardim from North Africa;[6] it forms a notable exception within the overall pattern of declining numbers (Wasserstein 1996: viii).

In terms of more recent immigrations (largely brought about for economic reasons), the Islamic communities are undoubtedly the most visible, though Britain also houses considerable numbers of Sikhs and Hindus. Islam is, however, the largest other-faith population in Europe, conservative estimates suggesting a figure of six million.[7] More specifically, Muslims make up approximately 3 per cent of most West European populations (Lewis and Schnapper 1994, Nielsen 1995, Vertovec and Peach 1997). The precise patterns derive very largely from colonial connections. The links between France and North Africa, for example, account for the very sizeable French Muslim community (3–4 million); Britain's equivalent comes from the Indian subcontinent (1.2 million). Germany, on the other hand, has absorbed large numbers of migrant workers from the fringes of South-east Europe, and from Turkey and the former Yugoslavia in particular. In the 1990s, the Muslim population has spread northwards – notably, for example, to Sweden (a country generously hospitable to political refugees from the Middle East). Finding ways to accommodate the growing Muslim presence in this part of the world is, in my view, one of the principal challenges facing twenty-first-century Europeans (and at all levels of institutional existence).

The presence of new religious movements in all European societies should finally be taken into account, not so much for the numbers that are involved (which remain minute), but for the issues that such minorities provoke. New religious movements disturb the European mind – whether this mind be secular, religious or sociological. For secular Europeans, new religious movements challenge assumptions of rationality; for the traditionally religious, they throw up disconcerting alternatives to Christian teaching; and for the sociologically inclined, they offer not only ample material for case studies, but more importantly, insights into the nature of European society itself – notably its capacities to tolerate difference. A glance, for example, at the website established by CESNUR (an Italian centre for the study of new religions[8]) will indicate the degree of controversy that such movements provoke and the difficulties faced by European governments (most notably the French) in coming to terms with them.

VARIATIONS ON THE THEME

So much for the commonalities of European religion within which the British will, I hope, recognise themselves alongside their European partners. But what of the differences? These can be conceptualised in a variety of ways. There are, first, the broad distinctions between the Protestant North and the Catholic South in Europe, with a variety of mixed types in between (The Netherlands, Germany and Switzerland). By and large the indicators of religious activity have fallen faster in Protestant Europe than in the South, though there are some suggestions (not all of them conclusive) that the Catholics will follow suit a generation or so later. In terms of religious activity, Britain falls squarely within the Protestant North, despite the particular nature of Anglicanism (it is both Catholic and Reformed) and the sizeable Catholic minority in mainland Britain.

It is equally important to remember, however, that certain countries simply fail to fit the pattern. Catholic Ireland, for example, may be part of the North from a geographical point of view, but Irish people are quite clearly very different from their immediate neighbours in terms both of denominational allegiance and of religious behaviour. Indeed the two parts of Ireland should in many respects be considered *sui generis* with respect to their religious identifications. The Republic is, in fact, very similar to Poland – both are cases where religion has become a form of cultural defence against external domination (in Ireland against the British and in Poland against, in turn, Lutheran Swedes, Lutheran Germans and Orthodox – or aggressively secular – Russians). This is the principal reason why the statistical indicators of Ireland and Poland are out of line with the rest of Europe; in both places 'religion' had (until recently) an additional job to do – it preserved the sense of a nation in face of external aggression, symbolic or real. A similar point will resonate in relation to South Korea (Chapter Five). Northern Ireland is, thankfully, a case apart; it will not form part of the following discussion.

Secondly, there are marked differences between European nations in terms of the variety of church-state relationships which have come into being in different places, mostly for particular historical reasons (Robbers 1996 offers a useful summary). We have already made the point that the common thread within West Europe lies in the existence of constitutional connections per se; the contrasts lie in the specificities of these relationships. Once again there is a broad contrast between Protestant and Catholic in this respect. In the Protestant parts of the continent (including Britain), ecclesiastical arrangements very often take the form of a state Church which embodies, in a benign form, national as well as religious identity. In these nations the in-dicators of religious activity tend, on the whole, to be low, but there is little evidence of hostility between Church and people, themselves largely of one mind. Indeed very positive relationships towards the state churches continue to exist – for example, in the Nordic countries, where residual membership of such churches remains astonishingly high (at least from the point of view of a British observer), despite the fact that attendance and assent to credal statements are some of the lowest in Europe.

In Catholic Europe, a rather different evolution has taken place. The extreme case is the French one. Here a strong and markedly clerical Church has for more than two centuries been involved in a series of confrontations with its alter ego, an equally developed and at times impatiently secular State, consciously embodying an alternative ideology.[9] Up to a point the same confrontations can be found in the Iberian peninsula and in Italy, but in both cases a rather different historical evolution has had a noticeable effect on the outcome. Spain and Portugal, for example, experienced dictatorship at a relatively late stage in

Europe's history – a fact which both compromised the Catholic Church, but also permitted a certain distancing in subsequent years. The Church, for instance, played a positive role in the rebuilding of Spanish democracy. The legacy of the past remains difficult to shed, however, and especially for the young who, quite clearly, are not attracted to institutional forms of religion. In Italy the presence of the Holy See appears to have made a difference to the capacities of the Church to maintain its institutional identity (not least, until very recently, as a bulwark against a strong Communist presence in Italian society).

The Greek case, finally, is unique. Greece is the only Orthodox country within the European Union, a fact explicable by the specificities of post-war history. Greek identity, moreover, is virtually indistinguishable from Greek Orthodoxy, rendering the position of religious minorities in Greek society extremely problematic. This is even more the case for Christian or para-Christian groups than for the Muslim minority in Thrace.[10]

SOCIOLOGICAL EXPLANATIONS

We need, now, to turn to the level of explanation. How is it possible to account for the religious situation that pertains in Europe at the beginning of the twenty-first century? A variety of approaches will be offered. The first is substantially a restatement of the secularisation thesis in its classic form and is based primarily on the work of Steve Bruce. The second, exemplified by David Martin, includes a much greater emphasis on situational factors – secularisation undoubtedly exists but takes place in different ways in different places (both within Europe and beyond). The final pair of explanations set out two very recent approaches to the situation in modern Europe (they include my own and that of Callum Brown – a social historian rather than a sociologist). In one way or another, all four approaches introduce the notion of 'European exceptionalism', the guiding theme of these lectures; all four, in addition, are considered with reference to the case studies that follow.

Until moderately recently, the secularisation thesis was considered axiomatic. Herein lay the explanation for religious decline not only in Europe but, in the fullness of time, in the rest of the modernised world. Such predictions derive from the central assumptions of the thesis itself: namely that there is a necessary connection between the onset of economic and social modernisation and the decline of religion as a significant feature in public (if not always in private) life. In setting out these connections, secularisation theorists draw both from the sociological classics and from the thinking of American social scientists, notably Talcott Parsons and Peter Berger at least in his early work (Berger 1967). In Britain the principal exponents of the theory have been Bryan Wilson (1982) and Steve Bruce (1996). We can take the latter as a representative case.

In *From Cathedrals to Cults: Religion in the Modern World* (1996), Bruce sets out the elements of the thesis with admirable clarity. The core of the argument lies in the changes that took place in Europe at the time of the Reformation when, for the first time, the authority of the medieval Church was seriously questioned. The challenge came in two ways – from a growing sense of individualism as the individual believer was freed from the mediation of the church in terms of his or her relationship with God, and from increasing rationality as innovative ways of thinking began to penetrate the European mind. For Bruce the two movements are necessarily related; both moreover are corrosive of religion in its traditional forms: '[I]ndividualism threatened the communal basis of religious belief and behaviour, while rationality removed many of the purposes of religion and rendered many of its beliefs implausible' (1996: 230). The first threads were pulled in the sacred canopy, which over time would unravel further and further – to the point, finally, of total disintegration.

Not everything happened at once, however. Indeed for the

religious pluralism ↔
religious vitality

following three centuries, religion remained a (if not the) central issue at the heart of European politics as nation fought nation over the right to control souls as well as bodies. Gradually, however, a modus vivendi emerged which allowed Europeans of different religious persuasions to live alongside each other, both within and between nations. Following the argument of the secularisation theorists, however, growing toleration simply poses another set of difficulties – both for the religiously committed and for the observing sociologist. These can be summarised as follows. If it is possible to tolerate a variety of religious views within one society, can any of these views be considered an embodiment of truth? In other words, once more than one 'truth' is permitted, *all* religions necessarily lose their plausibility, not to mention their capacities to discipline the faithful. Or do they? There are marked differences of opinion in this respect. It is these questions, moreover, that lead to one of the central issues in contemporary sociological debate: what precisely is the relationship between increasing religious pluralism (an essential part of modern living) and religious vitality?

Broadly speaking, there are two possible answers: one held by the rational choice theorists (see Chapter Two for a full discussion of this approach) and one by the defenders of secularisation theory, notably Bruce himself (1999). The argument turns on how the causal connections between the two variables are interpreted. Advocates of secularisation maintain that growing religious pluralism (historically associated with greater religious tolerance) necessarily undermines the plausibility of all forms of religious belief – thereby encouraging a greater degree of secularisation, manifested in indifference just as much as hostility. Following this view, religion becomes increasingly a question of options, life-styles and preferences, to the point that it loses much of its *raison d'être*. Rational choice theorists, however, argue precisely the reverse: religious pluralism enables the religious needs of increasingly diverse populations to be more adequately met – thereby encouraging rather than discouraging greater religious vitality. These questions will resonate repeatedly in the following chapters, notably the next. Quite apart from this, they immediately engage the issue of European exceptionalism, in so far as the outcomes appear to be different (markedly so) in different parts of the modern world.

Before developing this point in more detail, it is important to remember that Bruce is confining his argument to modern Western democracies – he is not including the religious movements sweeping across parts of the Islamic world or the serious disputes on the fault lines of the various faith communities that exist in the Near, Middle and Far East. But even in the modern West, there is surely, not only considerable diversity in the religious situations on offer, but seriously conflicting trajectories in terms of their likely development. Such contrasts lead naturally to the second set of explanatory theories, approaches associated above all with the work of David Martin (1978). In his seminal text *A General Theory of Secularization*, Martin lays considerably greater stress than Wilson or Bruce on the empirically observable differences between a wide variety of comparative cases, and the need to explain how the particular religious situation in each of these came about. It is clear, moreover, that advanced secularisation is more likely to develop in some circumstances than in others. It follows that there is nothing inevitable about the secularisation process – it may or may not take place, at different speeds, in different ways and with different effects. The contrasts between Europe (itself internally diverse) and the United States are central to this discussion. The difference between the two cases lies essentially in two very different religious histories, enabling in the American example a striking combination of economic modernisation and religious vitality, itself associated with a developed religious pluralism (a point discussed in detail in the following chapter).

How, then, did the secularisation theorists (largely of European origin) accommodate the markedly different American case? It is at this point that the notion of exceptionalism begins to resonate. The argument moves in two stages. The first stage embodies the notion of 'American exceptionalism'. In other words there are particular reasons for the religious vitality of modern America which require careful analysis – a subject that preoccupied scholars from different disciplines for much of the post-war period, Martin among them. Bit by bit, however, the argument has begun to swing in a different direction, encouraged undoubtedly by Martin's recent attention to the Latin American case and the emergence of Pentecostalism as a significant religious movement both here and elsewhere (Chapter Three). Observing the religious developments of the modern world (many of which have caught the sociological community by surprise), Martin – together with Peter Berger (1992) – have become increasingly convinced not only that the modern world (including large sections of the modern West) is 'as furiously religious as ever', but that it is Europe that should be considered the exceptional case rather than the United States. Berger has, in fact, moved full circle, from an advocacy of secularisation theory to a trenchant critique of this position.

Where, though, does this leave the question of European – as opposed to American – forms of religion? They must be seen, surely, as one strand among many which make up what it means to be European. European religion is not a model for export; it is something distinct, peculiar to the European corner of the world. What then has been the nature of this strand in the latter part of the twentieth century and what will it be like in subsequent decades? It is precisely these issues which have underpinned my recent writing on the religious situation in Europe.

Religion in Modern Europe: a Memory Mutates (Davie 2000a) brings together this thinking; it is concerned with the specificities of Europe's religious life and its relationship to European history and culture. In order to make these essentially Durkheimian links, religion is conceptualised as a form of collective memory. Such an idea derives from the work of a leading French

---

sociologist of religion, Danièle Hervieu-Léger, whose point of departure (Hervieu-Léger 2000) lies in trying to identify and to refine the conceptual tools necessary for the understanding of religion in the modern world. An answer gradually emerges in the definition of religion as a specific mode of believing. The crucial points to grasp in this analysis are (a) the *chain* which makes the individual believer a member of a community – a community which gathers past, present and future members – and (b) the tradition (or collective memory) which becomes the basis of that community's existence. Hervieu-Léger goes further than this: she argues that modern societies (and especially modern European societies) are not less religious because they are increasingly rational but because they are less and less capable of maintaining the memory which lies at the heart of their religious existence. They are, to use her own term, amnesic societies. Through what mechanisms, then, can modern European societies overcome their amnesia and stay in touch with the forms of religion that are necessary to sustain their identity? That seems to me the challenge set by Hervieu-Léger's analysis.

Religion in Modern Europe was largely a response to that challenge; the following paragraphs offer a brief summary of the argument. It must start, inevitably, with the churches themselves. Europe's churches have undergone a metamorphosis in the course of the last century.[11] No longer do they supply a sacred canopy embracing every citizen within the nation in question (in this respect I entirely agree with Steve Bruce), but nor have they disappeared altogether. They have become de facto, if not always de jure, influential voluntary organisations, capable of operating in a whole variety of ways – traditional as well as innovative. Placing the churches in the sphere of the voluntary sector or civil society is, in fact, the crucial point. In this sector of society the churches are key players; they are central to the structures of a modern democracy and attract more members than almost all their organisational equivalents. Churches, moreover, imply churchgoers (the social actors who carry and

the churches & Vicarious religion for Europe

articulate the memory). Who these people are in modern Europe and how they are placed in the nexus of social relations – an essentially Weberian question – is central to the understanding of both formal and informal patterns of religion in Europe and elsewhere. The data from an earlier section of this chapter provide a partial answer in terms of the European situation: these people are relatively well educated, often professionals, older on average than the population as a whole and disproportionately female.

A crucial concept begins to emerge from these analyses: that of vicarious religion. Could it be that Europeans are not so much less religious than populations in other parts of the world, but – quite simply – differently so? For particular historical reasons (notably the historic connections between Church and State), significant numbers of Europeans are content to let both churches and churchgoers enact a memory on their behalf (the essential meaning of vicarious), more than half aware that they might need to draw on the capital at crucial times in their individual or their collective lives. The almost universal take up of religious ceremonies at the time of a death is the most obvious expression of this tendency; so, too, the prominence of the historic churches in particular at times of national crisis or, more positively, of national celebration. Think, for example, of the significance of European churches and church buildings after the sinking of the Baltic ferry *Estonia*, after the death of Princess Diana or after the terrifying events of 11 September 2001.

This kind of argument works well for the European case, but less so elsewhere – a further argument in favour of exceptionalism. Here the *inapplicability* of the concept of vicariousness in other parts of the world (and especially to the United States) is the crucial point to grasp, a limitation easily illustrated from my own experience. I have travelled and lectured in almost every country of West Europe, frequently introducing the theme of vicarious religion. Despite the differences in language, it is extremely rare that Europeans fail to grasp what I mean by this term and to respond accordingly, more often than not furnishing me with innovative examples from their own experience. In the United States the situation is entirely different. Here there is no problem with language, but a far greater one in terms of cultural sensitivities. Quite simply, Americans understand neither the concept (vicariousness) itself nor its implications. Why should they given the entirely different evolution of their religious institutions?

The final approach to the place of religion in modern Europe is more circumscribed still. It concerns the recent work of a social historian and concentrates entirely on the British case. Callum Brown's *The Death of Christian Britain* (2001) attempts to explain the demise of Christianity in Britain in terms of a collapse of a shared discourse. In this respect the argument is similar to that of Hervieu-Léger despite a difference in vocabulary (memory and discourse are not interchangeable, but they undoubtedly overlap). Brown, however, goes further than Hervieu-Léger in that he identifies first the disproportionate significance of women as carriers of this discourse through the nineteenth and early twentieth centuries (exemplifying the argument from a wide variety of historical sources), but also the dramatic change that took place in the 1960s associated with the revolution in the roles of women more generally. No longer were women (and more particularly younger women) prepared to be the carriers of piety on behalf of the nation as a whole. The effects of this shift, according to Brown, have been devastating both for the churches and for the culture that they represent. Unsurprisingly (given both its title and its theme), the book has caught the attention of the wider public as well as the academic world.

In articulating his approach, Brown is distancing himself from Bruce and the classic secularisation theorists – secularisation in Britain, following Brown, did not really bite until the sixties, a controversial position that he underpins with extensive statistical data. It is, however, the historically central, but currently dimin-

Europe: The Exceptional Case

Brown —
the rôle of women + the death of Christian Britain in
the 1960s ??

ished role of women as carriers of the discourse that is of particular interest to *this* book, both with reference to Europe and to the comparative cases that follow (a remark that will resonate most strongly with reference to the chapter on Latin America – a part of the world where the role of women is again crucial but the outcomes very different). So much is helpful. Rather less so, in my opinion, is the stress on the role of women in Brown's work to the exclusion of all other factors. Even within the parameters of Britain, for example, he fails to explain why the obviously male-dominated institutions of secular society (notably the political parties and the trades unions) collapsed even more spectacularly than the churches and at precisely the same time. This widespread shift in social behaviour (both religious and secular) poses, in fact, a question that must be faced by all those interested in the recent decline in religious institutions: is the latter exclusively a symptom of secularisation or is it, at least in part, an indicator of underlying economic and social change?[12]

Both the question and some answers were addressed in some detail in my *Religion in Modern Europe*; they cannot be developed here. They need, however, to be kept in mind as we move beyond the European case and begin to set the material from the early sections of this chapter into its global context.

CONTRASTING CASES

This can be done in two ways – either by considering a range of global social movements which are essentially religious in inspiration or by using a geographical frame. In the following chapters, I shall be using the latter as a organising scheme. Before embarking on this enterprise, however, it might be helpful to say a few words about the former way of working. Both approaches (thematic and geographical) have implications for a theory that is primarily European in origin and both can be found in the useful collection of essays on *The De-secularization of the Modern World* edited by Berger (1999).

The three global movements that need to be taken into account are global Catholicism, popular Pentecostalism and the possibly overlapping category of fundamentalism (encompassing a variety of world faiths). All involve huge numbers of people – they are popular movements in every sense, but not in Europe. It is true that elements of each exist within the European context (both within and outside the mainstream churches) but none of them attract large numbers of people. Indeed, in the case of Catholicism, the global movement took off precisely at the moment when European expressions of Catholicism began to retreat almost to the point of no return – i.e. as the convergence between State and Church through centuries of European history became increasingly difficult to sustain (Casanova 2001). At this point Catholicism metamorphosed into a *trans*national religious movement, and as such has grown steadily since 1870 (the low point of the European Catholic Church). Most visible of all within this whole scenario is the person of the Pope himself, without doubt a figure of global media proportions. The Pope goes nowhere without planeloads of the world's media accompanying him, his health is the subject of constant and minute speculation in the international press; his global influence – whether approved or otherwise – is indisputable.

Global Pentecostalism is rather different in that its immediate impact is considerably less visible. Its effect on huge and probably growing numbers of individuals is, however, increasingly recognised, a phenomenon which is attracting the attention of growing numbers of scholars and in a variety of disciplines. The literature, as a result, is expanding fast (see, for example, the material brought together in Corten 1997).

Coleman (2001), Freston (2001) and Martin (2001a) offer state-of-the-art accounts of this phenomenon, each concentrating on a different dimension. Coleman, for example, is primarily concerned with 'Health and Wealth' Christians and

Global Pentecostalism

how they establish effective global communications, not least by means of electronic technologies. Freston concentrates on the political dimensions of evangelical Christianity, an aspect which is particularly difficult to discern given the fragmented, fissiparous and often apolitical (at least in a conventional sense) nature of the movement. Martin, in contrast, is concerned first and foremost with the cultural aspects of Pentecostalism, and more especially with cultural change. His book, like Freston's, is wide ranging, covering the diaspora populations of the Far East in addition to North America, Latin America and parts of Africa; both will become an important resource in later chapters. It is worth noting that Martin (in a developed theoretical chapter) pays particular attention to the absence of Pentecostalism as a widespread and popular movement in Europe. The notion of exceptionalism appears, once again, to be reinforced.

Fundamentalism(s) – whether in the singular or in the plural – is one of the most controversial concepts in academic discussion. One focus of this debate concerns the largely unresolved issue of whether a term that was used initially to describe currents of conservative Protestantism popular in the early twentieth century in parts of the United States can be helpfully transposed to a series of trends visible in a variety of world faiths some sixty or seventy years later. The fact that the terminology is difficult should not, however, detract from the evidence that these trends are indeed taking place – reversing in many ways the expectations of the Western (often European) observer, who assumed not only decreasing levels of global religiosity as the twentieth century drew to a close, but that such religion as continued to exist would manifest increasingly 'reasonable' tendencies.

That did not happen, at least not universally. What has happened – in different places and in different world faiths – has been the emergence of a range of reactive, conservative religious movements, resisting, in some cases, the modernising trends evident within the major faiths (modern biblical criticism, for example) or, in others, the incursions of modernisation (very

Fundamentalism

often associated with secularisation or westernisation) from the outside. Once again the scholarly literature is immense. A huge, and to some extent representative set of volumes (though not everyone would agree with its findings) can be found in the *Fundamentalism Project*, published through the early 1990s by the University of Chicago Press (Marty and Appleby 1995). For our purposes, one thread in particular can be extracted from this vast accumulation of scholarship: the range and location of the case studies which form the heart of the empirical project.

These case studies are taken from all the major world faiths and from almost all parts of the globe. What, however, is striking is – once again – the relative absence of examples from Europe. The three potential candidates are the following: traditional 'Lefebvre type' Catholicism, Ulster Protestantism and the Italian-based youth movement – Communione e Liberazione. In terms of the ideal-type of fundamentalism established in the project, however, none of the three fit the criteria completely or convincingly. The first is closer to traditionalism than a reactive fundamentalist movement, the second is more of a ethnic nationalism than a social movement and the last has been described by Italian commentators (Pace and Guolo 1998) as a 'fondamentalismo ben temperato'; it is, in other words, a partial illustration of fundamentalism, displaying some of the 'family resemblances', but lacking, in particular, any sustained reference to a sacred text.

So much for an approach based on three global religious movements, which could have provided the basis of three (at least) fascinating lectures. I have chosen instead to base my case studies on four global regions, with the specific aim of using each to highlight a particular aspect of European religion (or perhaps the lack of it). One reason for working geographically is to emphasise the fact that the 'rest of the world' is infinitely varied; it is not one place. Bearing this in mind, I have deliberately restricted the choice to Christian examples in an attempt to limit the number of variables that must be taken into account.

If we are to learn more about our own situation, it is important to select cases with more rather than less in common with our own. (This apart, the project is already sufficiently ambitious for a short series of lectures.) The four regions have already been mentioned: they are the United States (with some reference to Canada), Latin America, sub-Saharan Africa and three examples from the Far East – South Korea, the Philippines and (very briefly) Melanesia. They will, of course, cross-cut the movements already described, notably in the case of Latin America (where I have elected to emphasise the Pentecostal presence).

The way of working is essentially Weberian. It employs careful comparative analysis in order to highlight the significance of certain variables. One question will constantly repeat itself: what is it about West European society that makes it distinctive from a religious point of view if compared with most of the modern world? But a second follows on – inevitably, given the pervasive Eurocentrism in the relevant sociological thinking. Not only are Europeans increasingly distinctive in terms of their religious behaviour, they are visibly reluctant to admit this state of affairs. Such reluctance has important theoretical consequences, the essence of which can be found in Martin (1996a): Europeans assume *both* the normality of their own situation *and*, which is even more damaging, that the conceptual apparatus developed to understand a specifically European phenomenon can be used indiscriminately. In other words there is one conceptual map that can be taken on every journey; the fact that, figuratively speaking, this is a map of the Alps, which may not be all that applicable to the Rockies or the Andes, does not always occur to European scholars. Taking the wrong map, moreover, is more than unwise – it is potentially very dangerous indeed.

Hence the need for a developed theoretical discussion in the concluding chapter which returns to the idea of European exceptionalism from a conceptual point of view. It is concerned with two themes in particular. The first looks at Europe from the outside, isolating the specifically European characteristics that account for the religious situation in this part of the world. This discussion will have practical as well as theoretical significance for the churches, in that policies are more likely to be effective if they are based on an accurate diagnosis of the problem. The second theme is more ambitious: it is concerned with the study of religion in the modern world per se and the need to develop an appropriate set of conceptual tools (or maps) to carry out this task. It is this section that has been developed most fully since the completion of the Sarum Theological Lectures themselves.

AMERICAN ACTIVITY:
A VIBRANT RELIGIOUS MARKET

Attentive readers of the previous chapter will have noticed that
the earlier sections were, broadly speaking, divided between
those that described the parameters of religious activity in Europe
and those which sought explanations for these findings. This
distinction will be developed further in this chapter. It derives
from Runciman's *Treatise on Social Theory* (Runciman 1983/
1988) which splits the task of sociology into four distinct, but
overlapping activities. These are:

(a)   reportage – the gathering of data
(b)   explanation – accounting sociologically for the data
      presented in (a)
(c)   description – the term is used in a specialised sense
      (sociologically speaking) in order to describe how the
      situation 'feels' for the actors concerned
(d)   evaluation – including the possibility of policy making if
      this is felt to be necessary or beneficial.

Each of these categories will be applied in turn to the American
situation in order to establish a framework of comparison with
Europe.

Levels of activity

For European observers, one fact stands out above all the others in their observations of religion in the United States: that is the levels of religious activity. Approximately 40 per cent of Americans, for example, declare that they attend church weekly and even more once a month, figures which have displayed remarkable stability over several decades. Similarly, well over 90 per cent of Americans affirm that they believe in God, a markedly higher proportion than that found in most of Europe. Indeed, across a whole range of the EVS variables, Americans emerge as not only more religious but noticeably more orthodox (in the sense of endorsing credal statements) than almost all European populations (Ester, Halman and de Moor 1994: 37–52). Attendance and orthodoxy become therefore mutually reinforcing, exactly the reverse of what is happening in Europe.

A closer look at the attendance figures reveals, however, that not all Americans do what they say (Hadaway, Marler and Chaves 1993, 1998). If figures of reported attendance are set against actual attendance, a discrepancy appears in the findings – indicating, it is reasonable to assume, a significant degree of over-reporting on the part of many Americans. (Just how large these over-estimates are is a matter of sociological judgement and varies considerably between researchers.[1]) Over-reporting, moreover, whether large or small, raises important questions with respect to the data and the conclusions that can be drawn from it; these statistics need to be treated with caution. But even before the numerical analyses begin, it is important to ask why such a tendency exists in the first place. The answer lies in the following: Americans, it seems, are anxious to be seen as churchgoers, even if many attend less frequently than they say. Europeans have fewer inhibitions. Indeed the reverse, to some extent, is true – the over-zealous churchgoer may well run the risk of being called

Europe: The Exceptional Case

a hypocrite in Europe, especially in working-class communities (Ahern and Davie 1987).

Quite apart from the over-reporting question, there are, of course, marked variations in the American pattern (just as there were in Europe). Levels of attendance, for instance, vary from region to region in the United States: they are higher in the South and centre (in the Bible belt) and get progressively lower as you move North and towards the coasts. The difference in behaviour between men and women remains, however, a sig- nificant variable; women on both sides of the Atlantic are noticeably more religious than men, over a wide range of in- dicators and in very different types of churches. The age factor is more complex. It is true that young Americans leave their churches, just like young Europeans, and disproportionate numbers of younger people appear in the 'non-religious' category (Smith 1998: 80), but significant numbers of these individuals return to the churches later in life, complicating the overall picture (Roof 1993, 2000). Such variations are undoubtedly important and require careful and systematic documentation, but the crucial point is the following: even if the lowest (or at least lower) figures are used with respect to churchgoing in the United States, and even if the regional and other variations are taken into account, there is still a marked difference in levels of religious activity between America and most, if not quite all, European countries.

The difference between the old world and the new in this respect is, in my view, qualitative; it is not simply a question of degree. We have already noticed, moreover, that the reported figures are relatively stable (the actual figures rather less so), despite a certain amount of re-alignment between denomi- nations, or 'switching' to use an American term. Such re-alignment takes the form of a move away from the liberal Protestant mainstream towards more conservative forms of religion – notably varieties of evangelical faith (both black and

The USA

white). The proportion of Catholics in the population remains solid, despite a decline in mass attendance in the 1960s and 1970s (now rather more settled) – with this in mind Catholic churches appear on both sides of the switching equation. But taking the picture as a whole, there is in the United States, at least to some extent, growth to compensate for decline in the historically dominant denominations. In Europe, such decline is only too evident and in Catholic as well as Protestant constituencies, but there is no – or at least very little – compensating growth.[2]

A further point follows, more or less directly, from *both* the levels of activity *and* the growth in conservative Protestantism: that is the existence in America of the New Christian Right. Just like the estimates of religious attendance, the significance of this phenomenon has been disputed by American, and indeed British, scholars of religion (Bruce 1988, Bruce *et al.* 1995, Lienesch 1993), but the contrast between the United States and Europe remains, none the less, striking. In Europe there is nothing that can realistically be called a New Christian Right in the sense of a social movement of conservative Christians that has an effect on the political or electoral map of the nation in question, not least in the most recent Presidential election (Simpson 2000). It *is* true that a relationship exists between religious allegiance and political predilections in much of Western Europe – by and large there is a correlation between religious activity (of all forms) and conservative political leanings (Berger 1982, Medhurst 2000), but in ways that are very different from those that exist in America. It is also true that most European politicians would be wise not to offend too directly the religious sensitivities of both the minorities in their populations that do attend their churches with reasonable regularity and the very much larger numbers of nominal members. But the capacities of religious activists to lobby their governments over matters of policy is not a matter of concern (or from another point of view of approval) in most parts of Europe, whether these be evangelical Protestants in the North or Catholic political parties in the South. Indeed in Catholic Europe the restructuring of the political scene in recent decades has largely resulted in a loss of power on the part of the Christian Democrats. Why this is so is a story in its own right (it does not pertain only to secularisation), but it does indicate the incapacities of more conservative Christians to impose their will on the majority of citizens in terms, most notably, of uniform moral codes.[3]

An article which demonstrates the utterly different ways of thinking between European and Americans in this respect can be found in the quintessentially American journal *The National Interest* (Muller 1997). In this the author (President Emeritus of The Johns Hopkins University) not only draws attention to the fact that the New Christian Right does not exist in Europe, but implies that the European political scene is the poorer because of this. Following Muller, religion survives in America as a serious force in politics, not least in the form of a conservative religious movement – explicitly committed to traditional Christian values and vigorously opposed to social and political liberalism (including, amongst other things, the promotion of social justice through 'big government'):

> The key difference between Europe and the United States in this regard is twofold: nothing comparable to the American religious right is in evidence in Europe nowadays; and the liberal orthodoxy is institutionalized far deeper in the structures of the welfare state – and even inside the churches – in Europe than it is in America. This lay orthodoxy in under attack in America; in Europe, with the partial exception of Britain, it really is not. (1997: 35)

Most Europeans, of course, are profoundly supportive of the status quo in so far as it underpins social justice in the form of a moderately comprehensive welfare system (the principal theme of Muller's article); bearing this, and indeed many other reasons in mind, the absence of a religious right is for them quite clearly an advantage, not a disadvantage, something that many Americans (including Muller) find difficult to understand.

The place of televangelism is part and parcel of the same story. If the New Christian Right provides the political arm of particular forms of American religion, televangelism fulfils the same function in terms of the media. It is abundantly clear, for example, that televangelism resonates with a particular kind of Protestant Christianity that flourishes in North America, though more in some places than in others; its sociological patterns have been worked over by a variety of scholars employing a range of socio-political perspectives (Hadden 1987, Hoover 1988, Bruce 1990, Peck 1993). Unsurprisingly, these scholars conclude differently concerning the scope and influence of televangelism in American life. Hadden, for example, considers televangelism a highly significant social movement with ongoing influence in American life; Bruce, on the other hand, stresses the limited influence of televangelists outside their immediate and already committed constituency (this is a classic case of preaching to the converted). Such differences of opinion are important and need to be taken into account in an overall assessment of the phenomenon in question. Of a totally different order, however, is the more or less complete failure of the televangelistic enterprise on this side of the Atlantic, despite numerous efforts on the part of American evangelists to break into the European market (Elvy 1986, 1990, Schmied 1996).

This 'failure' has been covered in some detail in Davie (2000a). Essentially it revolves around the fact that the constituency with which the televangelists find a resonance in the United States does not exist in Europe and no amount of trying by means of increasingly deregulated radio and television networks can make good this fact. This is an area in which the power of the media has proved itself surprisingly limited, with the result that a European visitor to the United States, coasting the channels in any hotel room at almost any time of the day or night, is simply astonished when they discover the examples of televangelism on offer. Who, they ask, is watching this kind of thing? That person does not exist in Europe.

Modes of insertion

In terms of an overview of religion in the United States, a second set of issues concerns the manner in which religion inserts itself into American life – an area of enquiry in which data and explanation become increasingly difficult to disentangle (it is important to remember that these are indeed overlapping categories). In this section – and in order to present this issue initially in terms of data – I have relied heavily on Nancy Ammerman's magisterial work on *Congregation and Community* (Ammerman 1997), a key text for anyone wishing to grasp the essence of American life, never mind American religion. The dominant message of Ammerman's publication is not only the variety but the sheer resilience of religious congregations in American life, despite the many vicissitudes which some of them face. It is true that many of these congregations (perhaps the majority) face decline, whether in the long or short term (1997: 44), but even the Contents page gives an impression of persistence, relocation, adaptation and innovation in combinations that would be hard to match in Europe. There is, in other words, more of a forward movement here than would be possible in the old world and in an astonishingly wide variety of communities.

From a British point of view, an interesting comparison with Ammerman's work can be found (at least in microcosm) in a recently completed doctoral thesis, which examines both the growth and decline of religious congregations in Swansea (Chambers 2000). In this account, four case studies are selected to demonstrate different strategies of survival amongst different kinds of churches in a city undergoing a socio-economic metamorphosis as the port and industrial base retreat and new identities emerge. As in Ammerman's work, close attention is paid to religious ecology (i.e. the economic, social, demographic

---

and cultural environment of each congregation) and the many ways in which religious groups are able to relate to the surrounding community. The case studies are supported by a framework of statistics in a part of the United Kingdom where religious diversity has been more developed than in England; non-conformity has been an essential feature of Welsh community life for generations.

The crucial point to grasp in Chambers' study is the radical diminution in religious activity in the city taken as a whole, despite the examples of growth as well as decline in the congregations that form the principal focus of the thesis. The immediate past needs, however, to be set into a longer-term perspective. As the city of Swansea grew in the nineteenth century, religious congregations (especially non-conformist ones) established themselves in order to cater for the rapidly growing communities, alongside their secular equivalents – notably branches of the trade union movement and the associated political parties. Any analysis of the Welsh data must, moreover, acknowledge the fact that the factors that account for the decline of the traditional Free Churches on the East side of Swansea – the collapse of the close-knit working-class community centred on the docks – are precisely the same as those which account for the collapse of the trade union movement at the same time and in the same area. Both the organisations concerned with religion and those concerned with labour have lost their *raison d'être* – i.e. a community to serve whose common interests (whether religious or work-based) required institutional articulation.[4]

The striking thing about Ammerman's book and the American data more generally is that many *religious* congregations in the United States seem to have found creative ways out of these changing economic and social circumstances, unlike their European equivalents. This point is crucial. It should, moreover, be seen in relation to the wider, and politically urgent discussions of social capital that are currently taking place on both sides of

churches & communities

the Atlantic, a debate provoked very largely by the work
of Robert Putnam (an American political scientist).

Strictly speaking, social capital as a concept did not originate
in Putnam's seminal article 'Bowling Alone' (Putnam 1995); it
had already been used by a variety of authors to describe the
social ties that bind people together. Be that as it may, the notion
quite definitely caught the attention of both politicians and
public in the mid 1990s – Putnam's subsequent book of the same
name (Putnam 2000) has had huge media coverage. In this,
Putnam both documents (dramatically so) and expresses concern
about the relentless reduction in the membership of voluntary
organisations in American life, organisations epitomised by the
bowling club.[5] The churches, or to be more precise certain kinds
of churches, are seen as part of the same trend. The downturn
in the statistics (both religious and secular) in the later post-war
decades was both sharp and unexpected and has become the
cause of considerable public concern. Hence a burgeoning and
not always consistent literature on the nature and forms of social
capital and the precise place of religious groups in this.

The argument in terms of religion is complex even in
Putnam's own work. In his earlier, more historical, work on
Italy (Putnam *et al.* 1993: 107–9), Putnam seems to imply that
there is little connection between religion and social capital –
indeed if anything the institutional churches (and notably the
Roman Catholic Church) generate negative rather than positive
outcomes in this respect. In his analysis of America, in contrast,
the two variables appear not only to be related to each other,
but generative of positive consequences. Hence Putnam's
concern about religious decline in the United States, the more
so in so far as faith communities are arguably 'the single most
important repository of social capital in America' (2000: 66).
Those religious groups, moreover, that do continue to flourish
frequently exhibit inward- rather than outward-looking tendencies, i.e. they are less effective carriers of social capital than
those that are disappearing.

American Activity 35

Largely in agreement with Putnam, I would maintain that the connection between the two variables – religious activity and the generation of effective social capital – is likely to be contingent: in other words they are differently related in different social contexts. The context, moreover, includes the nature of the Church in question; the Catholic Church in southern Italy is very different from American denominationalism. But quite apart from this distinction, it is clear that certain kinds of religious organisations in the United States have been able to maintain their levels of activity despite the general trend downwards. Whether or not these forms of religion are, or are not, the most effective in terms of social capital is, I think, a somewhat different question to which different commentators will give different answers; it depends a good deal on how some aspects of American evangelicalism are interpreted (Noll 2000). For the time being it is sufficient to note that in Europe many forms of voluntary associations, *both secular and religious*, are finding themselves in the same, rather parlous situation. Cameron (2002) offers an interesting analysis of the British case.[6]

Why are the situations in Europe and the United States so different? The question leads immediately to the apparent advantages of a system based on *voluntarism* (the very essence of the congregations that Ammerman describes) compared with a relatively immobile state Church (the common feature of Europe's religious heritage), seeing in the principle of voluntarism the fundamental reason for the continuing vitality of religion in American civic life. The arguments surrounding this question will form a principal theme of the following section. At this stage it is sufficient to note that the independence of all religious groups from any kind of state support is, once again, one of the most striking features of American life as this is observed from across the Atlantic. Not only does this situation exist, it is, quite clearly, central to the self-understanding of Americans; it is an attitude that colours a whole series of subsequent issues, which relate not only to the constitutional issues

Europe: The Exceptional Case

of Church and State, but to the manner in which religion as such enters the public square.

One illustration of the latter can be found in the notion of civil religion, a concept famously developed by Bellah in the American context (Bellah 1970), but with roots in European political discourse (notably in the work of Jean-Jacques Rousseau). Bellah seeks above all to identify the features that bind Americans together. These include allusions to a shared Judaeo-Christian heritage (and here the connection of the two terms is crucial), emphasising in each case commonality rather than difference. Despite the formal separation of Church and State, phrases such as 'One nation under God' or 'In God we trust' continue to resonate throughout the nation. Such phrases are used judiciously by American politicians who wish to unite rather than divide their constituencies. They are, moreover, entirely compatible with organisational independence, in that no single Church or denomination is privileged above others.

Attempts to return the concept of civil religion to the European context have been made from time to time, in order, for example, to identify a civil religion of Britain or France.[7] The former – closely connected in this case to both established Church and royal family – is now under considerable scrutiny, partly in view of the vicissitudes of both Church and royal family, but more importantly given the developing emphasis on devolution in the United Kingdom. A further (and not unrelated) question at the beginning of the new century lies in the existence or otherwise of a European (as opposed to British, French or German) civil religion. What, moreover, might be its constituent elements in an increasingly diverse (religiously speaking) continent (Bastian and Collange 1999)? The logic of this argument leads however to further, somewhat disturbing questions: if the answer to the initial enquiry were negative, does it follow that the idea of Europe or of a European Union in any realistic understanding of the word, simply ceases to exist? Or to put the same point in a different way – do the diversities of

is there a European church?

modern Europe continue, despite everything, to outweigh the commonalities? The age-old sociological question concerning the relationship between economic factors (inevitably convergent if monetary union is to be taken seriously) and cultural forces is central to this evidently unfinished debate.

Increasing diversity

It is at this point that questions relating to immigration and the increasing diversity of religious life both in the United States and in Europe need to be integrated more fully into the discussion. In terms of the American case, new and significant data have emerged (indeed still are emerging) from a series of recent investigations in the field, notably the New Ethnic Immigrant Congregations Project (Warner and Wittner 1998) and the Public Religion and Urban Transformation work based in Chicago (Livesey 2000). Listening to recent presentations of this material by a wide range of American scholars, I have had the impression of an extending religious diversity – certainly not without its difficulties for many of the congregations concerned – but without the frequently present, and often oppressive, European factor of previous imperial connections. In some ways the questions are similar: how does a culture dominated for the majority of its history by Judaeo-Christian understandings come to terms with minorities whose values are rooted in an entirely different politico-cultural environment? But it does, I think, make a difference if that history is measured in centuries rather than millennia and in a country whose past (at least since the arrival of the first European settlers) has been dominated by successive waves of immigration from different parts of the world.[8]

The post-war shifts in the religious population of Europe, described briefly in Chapter One, raise questions of a different order. It is ironic that at precisely the moment when the historic religions in Europe are losing control of both the belief systems and life-styles of many modern Europeans, there should arrive

Immigration & diversity

in Europe representatives of religious communities from diverse (mostly pre-colonial) parts of the world, whose religious lives are far more tightly controlled, at least in the short term, than those of the average European. Religious pluralism, in this understanding of the term, is a crucial aspect of European life; it is largely dominated by the existence within Europe of approximately six million Muslims. In the final decade of the twentieth century, the episodes which revealed most clearly the failure to get to grips with the underlying issues that this new situation presents were (a) the controversy surrounding the publication of *The Satanic Verses* in Britain and (b) the *affaire du foulard* in France. Both are discussed in some detail in Davie (2000a) and both, to a large extent, remain unresolved. Hence, almost inevitably, the re-emergence of the underlying problems in the difficult circumstances following the attack on the World Trade Centre in September 2001.

Religious pluralism has, however, an entirely different meaning (in both popular and sociological discourse); it refers to the increasing fragmentation of belief-systems as a result of a further point made in Chapter One – i.e. the loss of control on the part of Europe's historic churches. Clearly this loss of control is more developed in some parts of Europe than in others (i.e. more in the Protestant North than the Catholic South), but it is evident all over the continent – a more or less direct result of the decline in churchgoing. As we have seen, such decline has not resulted by and large (and for the immediately foreseeable future) in large numbers of conversions to secular rationalism. It has, however, resulted in a growing diversity of religious belief, as the disciplines associated with regular attendance diminish and the market in spiritual goods continues to increase with the growing mobility of European populations. The New Age, itself extraordinarily diverse, is but one of the new spiritualities on offer.

It is interesting that recent work in the United States reveals a similar spiritual seeking (Roof 1999, 2000, Wuthnow 1999), *spiritual seeking / → specific religious institutions,*

despite – or alongside – relatively high levels of churchgoing. The context is different, however. For example, the links with organised religion are very much stronger in the United States, where seeking takes place within the churches as well as outside them and where specific forms of religious institutions emerge to meet the needs of the questing population. Once again the market is responding to demand and with considerable success.[9] Despite such differences, 'spirituality' as opposed to 'religion' becomes a category to be scrutinised by sociologists on both sides of the Atlantic, carefully distinguishing this understanding of religious pluralism (and the issues that it raises) from that which relates to competing, and relatively well-organised religious organisations. The confusion between these areas of study has led to persistent and damaging misunderstandings, not least amongst groups whose religious commitments form the very core of their existence and for whom a pick-and-mix, live-and-let-live kind of attitude simply will not do (Davie 2000b).

EXPLANATIONS

So much for a markedly different state of affairs on each side of the Atlantic in terms of reportage. How, then, can we explain these contrasts?

The first set of questions pick up a point already made both in the previous section and in the previous chapter: they concern the manner in which religion inserts itself into the wider society and how this relates to secularisation, a central and crucially important theme in the work of David Martin (1978). Broadly speaking, American religion cuts vertically into American society as each group of new arrivals brings with it its own religious package, and maintains or adapts this way of working as the generations pass. A glance round any American city, for example, indicates a huge diversity both within and between denominations: Irish, Italian and Polish Catholics (to name but the most

obvious) each have their own centres of worship and community
– now joined by increasing numbers of Latino congregations,
and Protestants (given their fissiparous nature) are even more
diverse. An essentially similar pattern is, moreover, continued as
different interest groups (in addition to national communities)
create and sustain forms of religion suited to their own particular
life-styles – a central theme of Ammerman's book.[10]

In Europe, in contrast, the insertion tends to be horizontal, a
pattern which derives ultimately from the collusions of religion
and power over many centuries, a direct legacy of the 'official'
status of Christianity as a state religion. As European populations
began, some more radically than others, to reject the political
dominations of the past, they discarded some, if not all, of the
religious connotations that went with these. The result, however,
is complex, a point well illustrated in the contrasts between
indices of religious practice and those of religious belief in most
of Western Europe. These contrasts formed a dominant theme
in the previous chapter, in which it became clear that an un-
willingness to attend a religious institution on a regular basis (all
too closely associated with the State in some places) does not
mean necessarily a parallel abdication in religious belief – though
it does alter very profoundly the context in which that belief
continues (or not) to exist.

The key sociological explanations for the contrast between
the United States and Europe can be found, however, in the
ongoing debate between the advocates of secularisation theory
and those who support the rational choice approach to religious
phenomenon. The former was discussed in some detail in
Chapter One, an account which stressed very strongly the *relatively* close fit between theory and data in the European case;
the trouble arose in exporting the theory indiscriminately, not
least to the United States. It is now time to outline the American
alternative in more detail.

secularisation / rational choice theory

satisfy human needs — at varying cost

Rational choice theory

Rational choice theory (RCT) is to America what secularisation theory is to Europe; indeed it has been described by some commentators as 'gloriously American' (Simpson 1990). It is a theory associated above all with the names of Stark and Bainbridge (1985, 1987), with important contributions coming in addition from Roger Finke (often in collaboration with Stark) and Larry Iannaccone. The debate concerning RCT (including a number of interesting case studies) has dominated the *Journal for the Scientific Study of Religion* in the 1990s. A further very useful collection of articles can be found in Young (1997).

RCT starts from the premise that the demand for religion in human societies remains constant. Being religious is part of the human condition, given the inability of individuals in themselves to meet many of their deepest needs (not least the security of knowing what happens to them after death). Hence the tendency to turn to 'compensators', which are substitutes for the real thing and which are provided, very largely, by means of religion(s).[11] Religious organisations offer to individuals rewards (certainty, comfort, fellowship, etc.) whilst exacting from them a corresponding range of costs (participation, conformity and money). Individuals choose their religions by weighing up rewards and costs, determining – for example – the degree of security that they will settle for weighed against the costs involved. Within such a framework, liberal forms of religion will offer less security than conservative ones, but at a lower cost.

Such a theory assumes the possibility of choice; it is, moreover, in the modern United States that the notion of religious choice is at its most developed, a fact amply illustrated in previous paragraphs. Conversely, the most obvious contrast to the market-based model of America – a point repeatedly stressed by the RC theorists – lies in the monopolistic (historically speaking) state churches of Europe, where, it follows, the lack of choice has severely depressed the demand for religion in any active sense.

market-based American
v. monopolistic European religious institutions

can RCT apply elsewhere than USA?

(The relative persistence of religious belief in modern Europe is interpreted by the RC theorists as additional evidence in favour of their theory.) Hence, on the one hand, the advocates of RCT critique, sometimes very severely, the concept of a state Church[12] and, on the other, they throw down a challenge. If a free market in European religion were allowed to emerge, there is no reason why the religious institutions in this part of the world should not flourish in the same way as their American counterparts. Secularisation in Europe is caused by deficiency in religious supply, not in demand. *99*

Unsurprisingly RCT has proved highly controversial. More precisely, there are supporters on both sides of the Atlantic, not least those in Europe – for example certain sections of the Church of England – who wish to break the ties between Church and State (see below). There are others, however, who are vehemently opposed and on two (overlapping) grounds. Firstly there are those, led by Steve Bruce (1999), who not only stress the increasingly secular nature of Europe and the failure of the RC theorists to come to terms with the realities of the European data, but – as we have already seen – attack the RCT protagonists right at the heart of their project. For the RCT supporters, pluralism and religious vitality are positively related; for Bruce the reverse is true. This was the point underlined in Chapter One. A second group of critics are primarily persuaded by the territorial limits of RCT; it is too American to be all that helpful in explaining patterns of religion beyond the borders of that country, whether in Europe or anywhere else, a point reinforced by Warner (1993, 1997). RCT may well be the new paradigm for understanding religious activity in the United States; its application elsewhere is noticeably more problematic.

My own position lies somewhere between the acceptors and the rejectors. I am not entirely persuaded by RCT if this is set out simply in market terms but I can see some merit in the approach. The crucial point to grasp is that Europeans, by and large, regard their churches as public utilities rather than competing firms; this is the real legacy of a state church history and inextricably related to the concept of vicariousness developed in Chapter One. As a result Europeans bring to those institutions an entirely different repertoire of responses from their American counterparts. Most Europeans look at their churches with benign benevolence – they are useful social institutions, which the great majority in the population are likely to need at one time or another in their lives (not least at the time of a death). It simply does not occur to most of them that the churches will or might cease to exist but for their active participation. It is this attitude of mind which is both central to the understanding of European religion and extremely difficult to eradicate. In my view it, rather than the absence of a market, accounts for a great deal of the data on the European side of the Atlantic. It is not that the market isn't there (it quite obviously is in most parts of Europe, if not quite in all); it is simply that the market doesn't work given the prevailing attitudes of large numbers in the population.

What I am trying to say, continuing a metaphor introduced in the previous chapter, is that a map of the Rockies (i.e. more rigorous versions of rational choice theory) has to be adapted for use in Europe – just like the map of the Alps (secularisation theory) for those who venture in the reverse direction. Such a map can, however, open up new and pertinent questions if used judiciously. I would, for example, be interested in its cultural as well as organisational applications, not least with respect to televangelism. Why is it that the European market fails to operate with respect to this particular form of religion? Or to put the point even more directly, why has it not been possible to *create* a market for this particular product? Is it simply the lack of a suitable audience (as suggested in the previous section) or is something more subtle at stake?[13] It might, in addition, be interesting to examine in more depth, and over a longish historical period, the relationship between capital and religion in Europe. In different historical periods this has been extremely strong (hence, for example, the wealth of religious art and archi-lecture particularly in Southern Europe – Tuscan examples come particularly to mind). Currently, however, the relationship is weak, or at least much weaker, though it is interesting to discover how much Europeans are willing to invest in their religious buildings at the turn of the millennium, even amongst Nordic populations where churchgoing is notoriously low (Bäckström and Bromander 1995).

DESCRIPTION

In many ways, this section of the enquiry (how does it *feel* to be a participant?) provokes the most pertinent questions of all for a sociologist trying to understand the nature of religion in different parts of the world. It is also the area of enquiry which is (a) most difficult to research and (b) most open to mis-interpretation.

My point of departure lies in an essay title that I set my undergraduate class in the sociology of religion: 'Is churchgoing *deviant* behaviour in modern Britain (or indeed modern Europe)?' Most students are capable of setting out the British/European statistics and of deciding that churchgoing is indeed statistically deviant – it is essentially a minority activity – but that it is more deviant for some people than others. In pursuing the latter point, students become aware of the patterns of religion in modern Britain/Europe and conclude that churchgoing is more deviant (and so differently constructed) for men than for women, for the young rather than the old and for working-class populations rather than the better educated. If they are dealing with comparative data, they could go on to make comparisons between different parts of the United Kingdom (noting the special case of Northern Ireland), between different European countries and, up to a point, between the different regions of England (or France) – the latter variations (and the French example is an especially good one) reflect contrasts established

church going as deviant behaviour?
men/women; old/young

over centuries, but still visible to the discerning eye. The persistence of local patterns of religious life forms an important part of this material, in that the meanings attached to actions can vary markedly from place to place.

But the key question lies elsewhere: that is in the interpretation of the word 'deviance'. I am repeatedly astonished by the sophistication of some students – few of whom are churchgoers – who scrutinise this term carefully and come to the conclusion that 'deviant' is an inappropriate word to use in this case. Churchgoing does not fly in the face of the values systems of European societies; in many ways it upholds them. And for the most part, Europeans are grateful to rather than resentful of the churchgoers who articulate in an active sense what many in the European population assent to passively (the precise meaning of vicarious religion). Quite what they are assenting to is not always easy to say: it has, I think, more to do with moral codes than with Christian theology. Be that as it may, there is a good deal of evidence to suggest that Europeans are not entirely complacent about the reduction in churchgoing in most parts of the continent in recent decades. Such an awareness revolves precisely round the realisation indicated in the previous chapter, i.e. that Europe is in the process of removing the 'keystone' in the arch of its value-system, without being altogether clear about what should be put in its place.

Two very different pieces of (British) evidence lead me to this conclusion. The first is an opinion poll carried out on behalf of the BBC in connection with a series of programmes on 'The Soul of Britain' (broadcast in the summer of 2000). For the most part the poll indicated a marked and unequivocal drop in the indicators of institutional attachment and credal statements compared with previous findings. So much was anticipated; rather less so was the fact that a significant proportion of respondents were not entirely happy about what was happening. To be more precise, 45 per cent regretted the decline in traditional religion, feeling that this makes Britain a 'worse' country. A very different

Why do Americans inflate/report their ~~_____~~ *church-go-ing?*

piece of work (Jenkins 1999) makes a similar, though not identical point. This is an anthropological account of religion in the everyday lives of English people. Despite radical changes in recent decades, the English still make a link between religion and 'respectability'. It follows that one source of respectability lies in connections (direct or indirect) with churches or chapels – it is not at all clear what might replace these as generators of social capital (to use Putnam's term) should the need arise.

It is now time to turn the question the other way round. What kind of answers would American students give if the same essay topic were transposed to the American classroom? It seems clear, first of all, that the statistics would lead some, if not all of them to a different conclusion concerning statistical deviance. In significant numbers of communities, it is clear that churchgoing remains the norm rather than the exception and not to go to church would be considered more unusual (or deviant) than going. In which communities/parts of the country this is so, is obviously central to the whole analysis. So too are the aspects of the question that relate to different kinds of people — men and women, for example, or different age or ethnic groups – from which it should be possible to build a demographic profile of the churchgoing population on both sides of the Atlantic (a useful comparative exercise) and the changes taking place in each case.

But in the United States, as in Europe, the real questions lie deeper – in the meaning of these actions for different groups of people. What does it 'mean' for representative Americans to attend church on a regular basis and how should we interpret their actions? Are the answers to these questions significantly different from those that emerge in Europe and how are we to research this difference? One way into this intriguing field of enquiry might be to examine in more detail the seeming propensity of Americans to inflate their levels of churchgoing as these are recorded in opinion polls. Why do they do this? At the very least they are answering similar questions in a different way from their European counterparts, who are, apparently, rather happier to declare their absence from the pews Sunday by Sunday.

The enquiry could, moreover, continue for a whole range of social actors present in the field. For example, given the very different religious situation in the United States, how does it 'feel' to be:

- religiously active
- a religious professional
- a politician with an eye to the electoral process
- a member of a religious minority – whether newly arrived or relatively well settled
- a journalist in the field
- a sociologist of religion?

I would like to take the fifth of these as a more developed illustration, drawing on Hoover's empirical study of religious journalism in the United States (Hoover 1998). Paradoxically, the striking thing about this case study is the *similarity* with European experience, despite the differences in levels of church-going between the two cultures. It is still, it seems, the case that most religious journalists in the United States feel marginal to the central enterprise of the paper in question. Or, as Hoover puts it, there exists a major mismatch between the worlds of journalism and religion in the United States just as there is in Europe, epitomised by the markedly areligious culture of mainstream journalists, if not always of the religious corres-pondents themselves. Also similar is the contrast between local and national papers (remembering, of course, the very different ways in which the press is structured in North America compared with some, if not all European societies). There is, I have to admit, no comparable empirical study of the religious corres-pondent in Europe, but the more anecdotal accounts of Longley (1991), Bunting (1996), and Defois and Tincq (1997) are, in the main, supportive of Hoover's findings. Their role is surprisingly similar to their American counterparts, more particularly in the recognition that even the most gifted religious journalists will be relatively limited in their impact if they do not have the support of the senior management of the paper.

I wonder, though, whether there might be larger differences between Europe and the United States in the response groups (as defined by Hoover): i.e. amongst the recipients rather than deliverers of the religious news. This is less likely to be the case with respect to the religiously committed respondents, but might well be so in terms of the wider – and in Europe significantly unchurched – public. But here there is no data concerning the European situation; it is, and must remain, simply a possibility.

EVALUATION AND POLICY-MAKING

I am hesitant to make *evaluations* about a society other than my own, but I have certainly heard Americans imply that, in the United States, there is too much of the wrong sort of religion. Noll (2000) certainly hints at this with respect to American evangelicalism. Unsurprisingly, Europeans rarely say the same thing, except sometimes with reference to Muslim and other minorities. Apart from a relatively small (though vociferous) group of secular rationalists, most Europeans, as we have already seen, regard their churches benevolently – i.e. as a necessary, and on the whole useful part of society. There are exceptions, The Netherlands being (or rapidly becoming) one of the most notable, where increasing sections of the population live outside the realm of the churches altogether, but they are relatively few. It is important to remember, however, that the exact nature of the attitudes displayed towards the churches varies across different European societies; such differences were discussed in some detail in Chapter One.

The following remarks regarding *policy-making* are necessarily selective; they are simply indicative of the kind of thing that is possible given the data and their interpretation already set out in this chapter. One example relates to the constitutional status of the Church of England. Amongst a number of committed Anglicans – disproportionately but not exclusively an evangelical group – covetous eyes are cast across the Atlantic where church-going levels are high. The lack of a relationship between Church and State is also noted, leading in some quarters to the suggestion that cutting the connections between Church and State in England might encourage a similar renaissance in the church-going figures at home. Such an argument, of course, fits perfectly with the understandings of the rational choice theorists. (Interestingly it is a position also supported by the liberal elite, albeit for very different reasons.)

My own view is that the situation is altogether more nuanced than these suggestions imply. There is, indeed, an important debate to be had in England about disestablishment, but it is not this one. And if it is one thing to cut the ties between Church and State, it is entirely another to eradicate the centuries of history that lie behind this, not to mention the accumulations of culture that go with it. I have already argued that the principal reason for the limitations of a religious market in Europe lies not in the lack of choice per se, but in the attitudes of Europeans towards the decision-making process itself. With this in mind, the cutting of the ties between Church and State in England might simply end in a double negative: you lose the advantages of establishment (which remain significant, if properly understood), but you gain nothing, or at least very little, in compensation.

One ongoing, and *partially* similar case study in this respect can be found in the Church of Sweden, which in 2000 did cut the formal connections between the Church and the Swedish State. It is important to remember, however, that the connections in Sweden were more developed than those in England and that the motivation for change was different. It is also important to grasp the relative wealth of the Swedish Church (given the church tax system); this was felt to be unjust in an increasingly,

You can't shed the history

the Swedish example

if modestly plural society.[14] With this in mind, the English and Swedish cases are not entirely comparable. The Swedish example will, however, be interesting to observe in the longer term – the more so in that it is the focus of an empirically based and sociologically informed research project which has the aim of documenting the various stages in the process and their implications for the Swedish citizen (Bäckström 1999).

An alternative focus in terms of policy-making concerns the religious minorities in modern Europe and the level at which the law should operate: should this be enforced at a European level or should it be the responsibility of the nation State? In this respect, one of the most interesting debates in recent years relates to the concept of 'religious' as opposed to racial categorisation in the legal system, a discussion with new resonance in the somewhat tense atmosphere that has followed the attack on the Twin Towers. The attempt, in the autumn of 2001, to introduce into British law an offence based on the incitement to religious as well as racial hatred is a case in point. Understandably the issue was of particular concern to British Muslims, who (unlike Jews or Sikhs) are unable to claim any kind of protection (or indeed privilege) under the race relations legislation. Such an absence is revealing; amongst other things it indicates a lack of understanding in some sections of both public and policymakers, each of which have difficulty comprehending that Muslims want to be considered as Muslims, not as (multiple) racial or national minorities.

It is interesting that the Muslim minority has been increasingly effective in raising the issue of a specifically religious identity in other ways as well, notably with respect to a 'religious' question in the national census (Fane 1999). The result was a typically British compromise: in 2001 a voluntary, and not very satisfactory, question was included in the census.[15] For the non-Christian populations of Britain, such a question represents none the less a step in the right direction.

My final point returns to the sociological study of religion

looser categories - not church-goers & non church goers
but converts / pilgrims

and concerns the outmoded nature of our measuring techniques. Very largely we continue to use static categories to measure increasingly fluid phenomena. We continue, for example, to divide our populations into churchgoers and non-churchgoers, as if this black and white distinction reflected current realities. For this reason, I am very attracted by Hervieu-Léger's recent work (Hervieu-Léger 1999) which introduces the much more mobile concepts of 'convert' and 'pilgrim': concepts which capture the mood of contemporary religious actors as they seek and search throughout their lives – with the intention of finding the particular religious package that suits them best. This, it is clear, is as true in the States as it is in Europe, but the framework is different. Europeans seek and search within the framework of their historic churches, more often than not returning 'home' when they die (Princess Diana being but the most celebrated example). Americans seek and search on a much more open market – a significantly different enterprise.

A NOTE ON CANADA – A HYBRID CASE [16]

The United States is not the only North American society. Why, then, has Canada moved increasingly towards the European rather than the American model in the configurations of its religious life? Canada, like Australia and New Zealand, represents a mid-point in a continuum of state or elite control versus voluntarism. In the mid-nineteenth century, the Protestant communities of English-speaking Canada were not so very different from their counterparts in the United States; the possibilities for voluntarism were, and in some senses still are, real. Such tendencies were, however, counterbalanced by the hegemonic Catholic identity of French-speaking Québec, a sub-culture which persisted until the 1960s when it collapsed dramatically – secularisation may have come late, but it came fast to French-speaking Canada. Notwithstanding such shifts, Catholicism in

Canada like Europe – because ?
(French) Res & Protestant established

general has played a far larger part in Canadian history than her markedly more Protestant neighbour, an important reason for rather different understandings of Church and State.

The consequence in Canada has been a declining establishment (notably in the Anglican and United Churches), an increase in the proportion of Catholics in the population, alongside declining rates of practice, and some movement towards the conservative churches – a pattern in some ways similar to the United States, but on an entirely different scale. There is, for example, no equivalent to the American New Christian Right (Noll 2000). What emerges overall looks increasingly European, despite Canada's new world status. Canada displays high levels of religious identification (for the most part with the historic churches), low (and declining) levels of religious participation, a limited rather than excessive pluralism and an increasing fragmentation of belief (O'Toole 1996, Bibby 2000). In short Canadians, like many Europeans, believe without belonging (Lyon and Van Die 2000).

LATIN AMERICA:
AN EXAMPLE OF GLOBAL
PENTECOSTALISM

The previous chapter ended with a note on Canada indicating that the Canadians were becoming less American and more European in their patterns of religious behaviour as the twentieth century drew to a close. In Latin America, paradoxically, the reverse seems to be the case. A religious pattern which in many ways mirrored that in Latin Europe for several centuries now appears to be moving, at least partially, towards the voluntarism of the United States. *Why* this should be so will form an important part of the following discussion, notably in the sections that offer explanations for the very dramatic changes that have taken place in religious life south of the Rio Grande.

With this in mind, this chapter will, at least in part, follow the distinctions in the sociological task that are already becoming familiar. It will start with a presentation of the data. There is a common agreement amongst those who are working in or commenting upon the religious field in Latin America that a profound transformation is taking place, namely the extra-ordinarily rapid expansion of Pentecostal forms of Protestantism. Strong terms are used: 'transformation', 'explosion', 'inexorable growth', etc., leading to 'overt, intense, and widespread competition between churches' in a continent once confidently assumed to be uniformly Catholic (Levine 1995: 155). These shifts will be mapped from several points of view, both quantitative and qualitative, and provide the take-off point for a whole variety of debates.

In the main such debates are concerned with an *explanation* for what is happening: how can we account for the dramatic shifts in religious behaviour in Latin America and where else in the world are these happening? The question is easily asked, but far more difficult to answer. An initial explanation has collapsed: it is increasingly clear that changes in the religious scene in Latin America do not depend on policies formulated or money accumulated elsewhere – more particularly in the United States. Alternatives, however, are more difficult to come by in a field characterised by ideological disagreement. Europeans, more-over – unaccustomed to rapid church growth – are particularly discomforted. Or to put the same point in a different way, here, as much as anywhere, are the inadequacies, or 'boundedness', of European ways of thinking exposed. How then can we (Europeans) grasp the significance of Pentecostalism as a wide-spread and popular global movement?

A final, but inevitable question follows from this discussion: why is the same thing – i.e. rapidly growing and popular Pente-costalism – not occurring in Western Europe? It is this issue that brings the chapter full circle, returning once again to the prin-cipal theme of these lectures: the exceptional nature of the European case.

FACTS AND FIGURES: THE CHANGING RELIGIOUS SCENE IN LATIN AMERICA

In many ways, it is difficult to comprehend the scale of the changes taking place. Latin America is a huge and diverse conti-nent with a population of almost 500 million people.[1] To say that approximately 10 per cent of this population is now Protestant (a percentage which is still growing) fails to convey either the size of the shift or the significance of what is happening. Some comparative data may be helpful. In Latin America as a whole, there are now about 45 million Protestants (the great majority of whom are Pentecostals). Between a third and half of these are Brazilian – i.e. some eighteen million. Compare this with church allegiance in Britain, where less than 10 per cent (five to six million) of the population are seriously active in *any* religious denomination and you begin to grasp the numbers involved in these shifts, remembering that most Protestants in Latin America are indeed active in their church allegiance (far more so than the great majority of Catholics). The same point can be put as follows: the Assemblies of God in Brazil, a single denomination, will easily outnumber the entire churchgoing population in Great Britain (Freston 1996). What is more these churches continue to grow; as the Brazilian demographic curve peaks and then falls (from the 1960s on), the proportion of Protestants goes on climbing.[2]

There are other, more local ways of conveying both size and significance. In Rio de Janeiro, for instance, between 1990 and 1992, a new church was registered every weekday, as a result of which '[i]n one Catholic diocese there were over twice as many Protestant places of worship as Catholic, and in the poorest districts the ratio was seven to one . . . The needier the district, the more Protestants: 20 percent in the poorest areas versus 6 percent in the rich South Zone' (Freston 1998a: 338). The attraction of certain forms of Protestantism to particular sections of the population appears almost limitless.[3] Miguez (1998) offers a similar account of Protestant expansion in a poor suburb of Buenos Aires. In Argentina the overall figures are smaller, but there is a similar process at work – all the more remarkable if compared with the evident reluctance of most local people to participate in more conventional forms of neighbourhood activities. Miguez puts this as follows: 'people were not eager to take part in political parties or community organisations. Contrastingly, the local Pentecostal churches were generating the more

spontaneous and dynamic forms of organisation and participation' (Miguez 1998: 1). Hence Miguez' decision to undertake
ethnographic research in this area. His title – *Spiritual Bonfire in
Argentina* – evokes the nature of the changes taking place; we
are a long way from fanning the embers of latent (some would
say moribund) Christianity in contemporary Europe.

Quite clearly something very significant is happening in a
continent which had been pretty uniformly Catholic for four
centuries. It is important not to forget this background, not least
the fact that 90 per cent of the population remain nominally
attached to their historic churches. There is also a need for
caution regarding the statistics as a whole. This is a part of the
world where plural practice has been widespread, not least
between popular forms of Catholicism and a variety of possession
cults, notably Candomblé and Umbanda, movements with more
or less close connections to African religions. Faced with this
situation, one of the most innovative aspects of Pentecostalism
lies in its attempts to break with what are seen as negative forms
of syncretism, creating instead a genuine pluralism with mutually
exclusive choices (see below). But old habits die hard. Religious
identity is far from static in Latin America; large numbers of
people move out of as well as into the Protestant churches,
making accurate estimates of membership all the more difficult.
There have, in addition, been crucially important shifts within
the Catholic Church itself, including both the emergence of
liberation theology and, more recently, increasing charismatic
tendencies. The relative concentration within this chapter on
Pentecostalism needs to be seen against a background of more
general change, exemplified in growing diversity within as well
as between the different denominations.

The regional variations within Latin America must also be
taken into account, just as in both Europe and the United States.
If it is clear that one variation on the European theme (the Latin
model with its hegemonic Catholic Church) became the pattern
exported to Latin America, it is equally plain that the model

implanted differently in different parts of the continent, a fact with continued significance for the spread of Pentecostalism. This has been 'easier' in some parts of the region than in others, the most propitious combination being a sustained latent religiosity alongside relatively low levels of Catholic control. Or, following Martin, 'the optimum conditions for Protestant expansion exist where the church has been seriously weakened but the culture not secularized, as in Brazil, Guatamala and Chile' (Martin 1990: 24). In Brazil it is the absolute number just as much as the percentage of Pentecostals that is so striking. Secular Venezuela and Uruguay are considerably more resistant, though Venezuela is now beginning to change. The initial chapter of Martin's overview *Tongues of Fire* maps, both geographically and sociologically, these very different, but highly significant trajectories.

Time as well as place is important. From an historical point of view the take-off point can be located in the mid-sixties, paradoxically at precisely the moment when the secularisation thesis peaked among Western sociologists. With this in mind, it was hardly surprising that Western scholars were slow to see what was happening elsewhere in the world, not least in Latin America; quite simply they were looking in the wrong direction for the wrong kind of evidence (Martin 1996a). South of the Rio Grande, however, two things were occurring more or less simultaneously in this pivotal decade. The size of the Protestant community began to expand exponentially and the nature of the Protestant churches altered; they ceased to be small, missionary based and in some senses liberal (in terms, for example, of their economic and social critique) and became instead much more like a mass movement, increasingly indigenous and increasingly dominated by Pentecostal (somewhat apolitical) tendencies. In assessing this shift, the influence of the United States in the form of American missionaries and American money became, inevitably, a crucially debated point. It will be discussed in more detail in the following section.

Soup American ?

It is important, finally, to consider what is happening in terms of 'rival civilisations' (Martin 1990). Following Martin, Latin America looks as though it is becoming rather more like the American market described in Chapter Two and rather less like the Latin model exported from Europe some four centuries ago. How such a shift is conceptualised depends a good deal on how you feel about the alternatives in question. For some observers, incipient patterns of American-style religion (whether these are imposed from outside or freely chosen) are seen as a particularly insidious form of cultural imperialism; for others, this is a way of liberating not only the market but the individual, now able to make choices with hugely important implications for life-style. No wonder the controversies that follow are heated as well as complex.

An ethnographic example

One way of conveying both the complexity and the nature of Latin American Pentecostalism is to look in more detail at one particular case. Rowan Ireland's *Kingdoms Come: Religion and Politics in Brazil* (1991) offers an excellent example. In this, Ireland covers the entire religious scene of a small town on the periphery of greater Recife in North-east Brazil; in other words he describes not only the Pentecostals (the *crentes*) but the Afro-Brazilian spiritists and the Catholics as well. But in each case, the first introductions are to a range of individuals, in a series of extended interviews, who demonstrate the differences as well as the commonalities of the various religious movements covered in the book. So we meet Severino, Teresa and Zé, then Valdo and Madalena, each of whom demonstrates something different about Pentecostalism. Only then are the rituals of church and sect described and, eventually, the particular impact that these people have on the local political scene. Theories about religion and politics (drawing on a series of comparative studies) come last and to some extent least.

varieties of crentes

As the bigger picture gradually emerges, we are able to appreciate the subtleties within Pentecostalism and the dangers of generalisation. There is, for example, the distinction between church-centred *crentes* and more sectarian *crentes*, in their very diverse attitudes both towards political culture in general and towards the political life of the community (1991: 93–7). With this in mind, Ireland is able to make better sense of the ambiguities and conflicts within the literature on Pentecostalism in Brazil (and indeed elsewhere). His informants interrogate the emergent theories in a series of imaginary dialogues (1991: 102–8), a constant reminder that theories which fail to take individuals into account are unlikely to be fully satisfactory. The plea that Pentecostals should not be stereotyped (conversely that they are diverse and real) should be born in mind throughout this chapter, not least in the following section.

EMERGENT DEBATES

Why did it happen?

The first of these debates is the most difficult (for the reasons set out in the introduction to this chapter) and centres on why such a significant shift has occurred at all. Bearing in mind the unavoidably ideological nature of this discussion, it is wise to recall at the outset the sheer scale and variety of the religious field in Latin America and, following Ireland, of Pentecostalism itself. Given such potential, it is most unlikely that one reason, or even several reasons (grouped into neat and tidy themes), will emerge to account for something so diverse. Freston (following Droogers 1998) is undoubtedly right to draw attention to this point:

> Pentecostalism is flexible and there is unlikely to be a single grand reason for its success. An eclecticism based on the ambivalence of religion must take into account not only

political and economic, but also social, cultural, ethnic and religious factors; not only the macro level (which social characteristics favour conversion) but also the micro level (why only some people with those characteristics convert); not only the appeal of Pentecostalism to men but also (especially) to women; not only the demand side (why people are ready to convert) but the supply side (what Pentecostals do to maximize their potential public). And it must ask not only why Pentecostalism grows so much, but why does it not grow more, and why some types grow more than others. (Freston 1998a: 347–8)

The following paragraphs will seek to do justice to some of these issues despite the obvious limitations of space.

It is easy to see, first of all, how several strands in the debate become entangled. For example, from the point of view of the Catholic Church, and especially those who have invested whole lives in confronting the appalling economic and social conditions of rapid urbanisation, it is important to find a reason for the apparent predilection of substantial numbers of poorer people for Pentecostal congregations rather than their Catholic equivalents – the base communities of liberation theology. That reason can be found, at least in part, in the notion of an external manipulation of the religious scene, in which American missionaries (unwittingly or not) become the agents of American imperialism, opposed not only to the leftist leanings of liberation theology but to its supposed collusion with suspect regimes. It is this paradigm, however, that can no longer be sustained in that it fails to offer a convincing explanation of what is obviously and increasingly an indigenous movement of Latin American people.

A rather more *self*-critical, but none the less Catholic variation on the theme can be found in a discourse which locates the crucial explanation for what has happened in the immobilism of the Catholic Church itself – a heavily institutionalised, top-down

why? Pentacostalism rather than liberation theology? v the immobilism of RC

freely made choices of ordinary people

clerical structure which, despite *basismo* (the base communities), cannot adapt fast enough to the changes taking place on the ground (Levine 1995). Yet another strand (this time favouring indirect, if not direct American influence) stresses the indigenis- ation of Latin American Pentecostalism – congregations take off when missionaries leave, not the other way round – but in forms that require submission to a leadership, which in style (if no other way) are reminiscent of American evangelists, a point reinforced by media replications of American televangelism.

A very similar set of narratives can be presented sociologically rather than pastorally, in terms, for example, of the structural changes taking place in Latin America, the conservatism of the Catholic Church, the seductions of American culture and the vulnerabilities of the population to external influence. But either way (i.e. whether the discourse be sociological or pastoral) a debate emerges which not only pays insufficient attention to the *multiplicity* of causes already pointed out by Freston, but also – and crucially – to the freely made decisions of ordinary people. Conditions are invoked which explain why large numbers of people have moved from one set of allegiances to another, but which fail in many cases to take into account (a) the motives of the people themselves and (b) why significant sections of the population do not make the same choices.

Martin's analyses (1990, 2001a) overcome some of these difficulties – notably the tension between external pressure and internal choices. American contacts, American culture, indeed Americanism itself, are attractive in so far as they are outward looking, English-speaking and corrosive of the organic union between faith and community whether at national or at tribal level (Martin 1990: 107). They are representative of modernity, global connections and economic prosperity. In this sense Pente- costalism looks up and out and becomes part of a global transformation. But it also provides a safe-haven, freely joined but firmly directed (hence the leadership style) in which dis- advantaged people, if they so choose, can find both mutual support and a sense of self-worth (individually as well as collectively) as members of a redeemed community. Significant changes in life-style occur in consequence. In order to 'work', it seems that Pentecostalism needs at one and the same time to be externally linked and firmly bounded; features which appear at first to be mutually exclusive turn out, on closer inspection, to be mutually supportive.

The stress on the individual believer is important. Mariz (1990, 1994), for example, compares Pentecostalism, Catholic base communities and Afro-Brazilian spiritism in Brazil paying particular attention to the effects that these movements have on people who live in poverty. Pentecostalism has, she argues, a particular appeal to the poorest of all, providing psycho-social and cultural means to avoid the mentally damaging consequences of extreme poverty — in other words, it provides a bulwark against the kinds of activity that aggravate destitution (alcoholism, domestic violence and economic fecklessness). The consequence of conversion is partial if not dramatic improvement in economic circumstances, reversing the likelihood of a downward spiral. A sense of order (sanctioned at times by divine intervention) begins to replace the chaos of everyday life, leading to constructive rather than destructive behaviour, a point that will emerge again and again with reference to both economic and family life.

This kind of discussion edges towards a second and equally problematic set of issues: those concerned with an appraisal or evaluation of Pentecostalism (in the sense that these terms were described in Chapter Two). It is at this point, moreover, that the different perspectives of the various commentators are at their most apparent.[4] For example, if it is clear, on the one hand, that almost all observers link the growth in Pentecostalism to the processes of modernisation, and especially to the dislocations of rapid urbanisation that have characterised recent Latin American history, there is markedly less unanimity when it comes to the likely outcomes of this situation. Bastian (1992, 1994), for instance, supports the argument first outlined by Lalive d'Epinay

(1969, 1975). Both authors stress the at best neutral, but at worst more negative effects of Pentecostalism vis-à-vis social consciousness or political intervention. Reform is hindered rather than helped by communities that are not so very different, de facto, from traditional forms of Latin American religiosity (which embody above all stultifying methods of social control and subordination). Indeed Bastian goes so far as to ask whether Latin American Pentecostalism is really 'Protestant' at all; its real affinities lie, he argues, in Latin political culture rather than in the democratic ideals of historic, presumably Calvinistic, forms of Protestantism.[5]

Martin, in contrast, is more inclined to follow Willems (1954, 1964, 1967); in this case both writers are more optimistic in terms of the future. In Martin's analysis, for example, Pentecostalism offers a form of religion quintessentially suited to the rapidly modernising society – and not only in Latin America (hence its success). More than this, Pentecostal communities offer training in democratic values, just as the earlier waves of Protestantism did in both Europe and North America (in other words, they are generative of positive social capital). For Martin the genealogy of Pentecostalism is of paramount importance; for him, it is the natural successor – in a lineage of 'voluntary, fissile and participatory' forms of religion (1990: 5) – of Puritanism (Mark 1) and then Methodism (Mark 2). The importance of Pentecostalism (Mark 3) lies in the fact that this is the first time that Protestantism, or Protestants, cross the Rio Grande in significant numbers. An additional point follows from this; once a particular form of religion (or to use Weber's term a religious ethic) finds a conduit, or series of conduits, through which to pass, the role of the missionary very largely becomes obsolete. The relationship with conservative American churches is no longer necessary to Pentecostal expansion (that takes place with a momentum of its own), but – as we have noted – remains highly significant as a symbol of American culture seen as a whole.

Freston (2001), finally, repeatedly insists on the sheer diversity

in the democratic lineage of Puritanism & Methodism?

of Pentecostalism in Latin America, and indeed elsewhere. With this in mind, more than one thing (positive and/or negative) can be happening at once – a point that will resonate even more strongly with reference to the economic and political implications of the changes that are taking place. New forms of religious life will emerge, moreover, which are specific to the Latin American case; they will not (and cannot) be replicas of what is found elsewhere – in Europe or the United States, for instance. Hence, surely, an even greater need for innovative theoretical models to understand fully what is happening in large parts of the developing world.

The relationship with liberation theology

Some reference to liberation theology has already been made. Following Mariz, for example, it tends to attract groups of people who have some education and whose economic situations are slightly less critical than many Pentecostals. Despite such distinctions, however, it is clear that the base communities of liberation theology and the ever-growing number of Pentecostal churches are inhabiting much the same social space – a situation bound to provoke tension. It is now time to expand this complex and difficult relationship.

Lehmann's work is particularly significant in this respect (Lehmann 1996). As a scholar of Latin America for some thirty years, Lehmann failed initially to take the religious factor into account at all. The first step towards remedy led to a study of liberation theology and base communities with respect to both economic and political (democratic) development (Lehmann 1990). By the time, however, that the author came to do detailed fieldwork in Brazil in the early 1990s, it was clear that the presence of Protestantism demanded equal attention in terms of empirical investigation. What emerges, in consequence, is a developed analysis of the religious field in Latin America, envisaged as an arena in which contending forces 'struggle for the spirit' (hence the title of the 1996 book). Macro as well as micro questions come to the fore:

MM

> The big questions are very big: do the people feel more faithfully represented by, or identified with, the revolutionary priests and nuns in their jeans and sandals, promising a long period in the wilderness travelling towards an uncertain Promised Land, and offering a diet of agonized self-questioning, of seminars and consciousness-raising combined with mini-projects, to sustain the People of God on their journey? Or will they be drawn towards the pastors, uniformly respectable in their suits, white shirts and black ties, as they proclaim the tangible happiness that will follow from a fulminating conversion experience, a herculean effort to get their lives and their families under control, and the financial discipline of a weekly contribution to church funds? (Lehmann 1996: 3–4)

Catholic base Communities ties or P. Con- version

The research questions that follow operationalise these ideas, contrasting the 'option for the poor' articulated by liberation theologians with the 'options of the poor' in the form of individual choices in favour of Pentecostalism. Each possibility – the membership of a base community or Pentecostal conversion – is set out in terms of its relationship to the history, culture and institutions of Latin America in general and of Brazil more particularly. Theme and counter-theme are repeatedly set against one another: one modality, for example, seeks insertion into the highly valued culture of the people (the Catholic mode of inculturation); the other continually confronts what are construed as the evils of local behaviour (i.e. the feasts, celebrations, rituals and rhythms to follow Lehmann's own list), offering the convert a new and 'better' way. The stakes, quite clearly, are very high indeed, a matter – no less – of life and death.

A second attempt to 'compare and contrast' these two powerful movements can be found in the final volume of the University of Chicago's Fundamentalist Project.[6] In this account, there is a stronger emphasis on the commonalities of liberationist

Similarities

Catholicism and Pentecostal Protestantism, in so far as both movements share an agenda 'built around literacy, small and intense groups, flexible organization, and emphasis on personal as well as community responsibility' (Levine 1995: 162). Both, moreover, are working in the same economic and social context, and both reach out to particular demographic categories. Core differences remain none the less; for Levine these reside in the structural contrasts between Catholicism and Protestantism. Protestantism has a freedom to innovate denied to the Catholic Church, not least the freedom to create new and autonomous churches as the need arises. The fissiparous nature of Protestantism, though problematic at times, necessarily engenders flexibility, a valuable quality in times of rapid social change.

The second part of Levine's essay raises rather more analytical points concerning the applicability of the term 'fundamentalism' to the changes taking place in Latin America. A significant step in the argument turns on the apparent similarities between the emergent Pentecostal churches of South and Central America and conservative Protestant groups in the United States (an argument reinforced by the supposed influence of American money and manpower in Latin America). On closer inspection, however, such similarities turn out to be spurious, prompting, in turn, a reconsideration of the concept 'fundamentalism' and its applicability to the Pentecostal case. Pentecostal forms of religious life south of the Rio Grande do not on the whole display the 'family resemblances' or common features of fundamentalism as these are set out in the Chicago Project, prompting an inevitable and considerably more searching question. If existing terms and concepts do not enable us to see clearly what is happening in the religious field in this (and indeed other) global regions (see note 6), we need to think carefully about alternatives – a major theme in the concluding chapter of this volume.

Two questions conclude this short section. Both should be considered within the framework of European exceptionalism.

---

is P 'fundamentalist'?
– drawing on American 'conservatism'

Why is it that liberation theology and its associated base communities are frequently viewed with sympathy in Western intellectual circles, whereas Pentecostalism is not? And does this distinction tell us more about the commentators than about the phenomena that they are supposed to be observing?

A transformation in gender roles

Most accounts of Pentecostalism in Latin American both set out the statistics of extremely rapid growth and urge caution in their interpretation. On one point, however, all the commentators *the attraction for women* agree: this is a movement disproportionately attractive to women, despite the presence of men in leadership roles. Why should this be? To a certain extent the same paradox confronts the observer of European forms of religion (Francis 1997, Walter and Davie 1998). In this respect Europe is, it seems, similar to rather than different from other global regions. The explanations (*why* women behave differently from men), however, are different in each case;[7] so too are the outcomes – markedly so.

Brusco's pioneering work in Colombia provides a useful starting point for the Latin American material. Brusco rejects the relatively simplistic notion that significant numbers of women are attracted to Pentecostal churches to compensate for the lack of fulfilment in secular life. Her analysis probes at a much deeper level in that it emphasises the transformation of gender roles (i.e. of both men and women) brought about by conversion. The effects are tangible:

> My data on Colombian evangelical households supports the conclusion reached by other analysts of Latin American Pentecostalism: that conversion of both a woman and her spouse improves the material circumstances of the household. Quite simply, no longer is 20 to 40 percent of the household budget consumed by the husband in the form of alcohol. Ascetic codes block many of the other extrahousehold forms of con-

good for the household   [*cf St Cs in 1890s*]

sumption that characterize masculine behaviour in Colombia, such as smoking, gambling and visiting prostitutes. (Brusco 1993: 147)

Keeping one household – the consequence of marital fidelity – moreover, is considerably more economical than keeping two (or more).

The core of Brusco's account resides, therefore, in the effect of Pentecostal conversion on both male and female behaviour, a shift which results in a redrawing of the boundaries of both public/private and male/female roles. Most notably, the men withdraw from the street and assume, alongside their wives, responsibilities in both the church and the home (in other words in the private realm). With the new roles in place, the relative asceticism of Pentecostal teaching leads to modest upward mobility (or at the very least a more secure economic existence) and, crucially, to education for the children – itself a decisive factor in inter-generational mobility. The household becomes an effective corporate group. The fact that this analysis does not meet the criteria of Western feminists in terms of 'liberation' is immaterial. It works in practice, an undeniable attraction for the women concerned.

Lehmann (1996) also concentrates on conversion. The accounts of this experience given by women are primarily concerned with physical and psychological illness, whilst those of men concentrate on social and moral failings. The need to escape from the latter is paramount for men. Once escape is achieved, however, the crucial formula is in place: in Brazil as much as in Colombia, bringing the husband under control is synonymous with healing the family. The fact that the women describe this process as bringing the men under control and the men describe it as self-control is, once again, of little importance; either way an escape route is discovered, which frees men from the classic Mediterranean or Latin stereotype (a circulation between partners in a series of unstable relationships). In other words, Brusco's findings are reinforced by Lehmann: following conversion, *machista* behaviour diminishes and the nuclear (rather than the extended) family becomes the effective unit of organisation.

Maldonado, finally, comes to the same conclusion. Pentecostalism provides 'a theologically informed domestic conservatism' (1993: 234), which both counters traditional male behaviour and offers, in consequence, security to women and children – by means of increasing affection, responsibility and leadership. The last of these is important: the man remains squarely head of the household (hence the dilemma for Western feminists). In concentrating their efforts at this level, Pentecostal churches have, however, met an evident need, the consequences of which spill over into other aspects of life, not least the economic sphere.

Economic and political implications

The transformation in family life already described is the key to economic change. Add to this the fact that groups of families form networks of reciprocity, trust and community values – essentially economic virtues – and it is not difficult to understand the cumulative effects of Pentecostal conversion. This is not, it is important to recognise, a question of hard-headed capital accumulation; nor is it a direct application of the Weber thesis. It is a considerably more modest enterprise. But given the precariousness of the economic context more generally, the very basic qualities of honesty, thrift, self-discipline and organisational skills stand out. In consequence, as people move from the countryside into the city looking for better jobs and educational opportunities (especially for their children), Pentecostal communities become 'havens and way stations in the journey up the socio-economic ladder' (Maldonado 1993: 235).

The long-term effects of what is happening remain uncertain. Berger, in his introduction to Martin (1990), is optimistic, feeling that all the elements of the 'Protestant ethic' are now in place and it is only a question of time before they exert their influence *economic betterment → the prosperity gospel*

on economic life. Martin himself discusses the same possibility, but underlines very firmly the complex nature of the original thesis – this is no one-to-one causal relationship (Halévy in fact is as important as Weber). Martin remains, however, cautiously convinced at least at the level of potential: an attitude of self-worth can be realised economically as well as spiritually. Others are less sure. Freston (1998a, 2001), for example, reviews what can only be described as ambiguous evidence, stressing the fact that even if the work ethic is indeed reinforced by Pentecostal lifestyle, the economic and social conditions are so markedly different from those in early modern Europe that the outcome cannot be anything but uncertain. For Levine and Stoll (1997), it is simply too soon to say, a fact which is as true for the long-term consequences of liberation theology as it is for Pentecostalism.

A further, rather different point should be noted in conclusion – the gradual encroachment of a prosperity gospel as Pentecostalism creeps up the economic scale. This is an attractive option for the relatively well-off, but one which necessarily disrupts the pattern of upward social mobility. You cannot at one and the same time affirm material comfort (in the sense of well-being) and appeal to a sense of anguish (regarding salvation) as a principal source of economic motivation. The prosperity gospel has, moreover, a bad press – rightly so in many ways, particularly if turned on its head to condemn the less successful or less healthy as necessarily faithless or unbelieving. Having said this, the line between betterment and prosperity is a very fine one: the former (almost universally applauded) is almost bound, if taken seriously, to lead to the latter.[8]

Rather similar tensions can be found in the literature concerning the political outcomes of Pentecostalism. The question is highly controversial – unsurprisingly given the nature of Latin American politics, a part of the world where the experience of democracy is both limited and short-term. The supposed juxtaposition with liberation theology is a further complicating factor; so too the assumption that withdrawal from the political field is necessarily an endorsement of the status quo – the more so if this is reinforced by a theologically inspired respect for the currently ordained powers, themselves mirrored in patterns of church life. It is difficult, finally, to escape entirely from the stories of corruption and scandal that from time to time pervade Pentecostal (just like any other) dealings with the world (Freston 1998b: 43–4). All of this, it might seem, adds up to a negative rather than positive portrayal of Pentecostal political leanings.

What can be said on the other side? There is at least the possibility (indeed the probability, following Martin), that the creation of a free, or at least freer space for particular forms of religious life will have a similar – and democratising – effect on the political field. The process takes place as follows. In so far as Pentecostals reject the status of a minority and syncretic religion under the general protection of the Catholic Church (in marked contrast, for example, to the attitude of the possession cults), they demand a new type of religious pluralism in the form of equal rights for all religions before the State. Or to put the same point more analytically, the breaking of the monopoly or corporate union between Church and State may turn out to be of crucial political significance, despite or perhaps precisely because of the exclusive, at times apolitical and seemingly intolerant claims of the Pentecostal sector. In this respect it is crucially important to distinguish between the short and long term, a point that will re-emerge in the discussion of Pentecostalism in Africa.

The seeming intolerance of Pentecostals may be effective in other, more immediate ways, an attribute exemplified in antipathy towards various forms of social evil – notably pervasive urban violence. Such evils demand confrontation and at all levels of society (Birman and Pereira Leite 2000: 274); quite clearly they are corrosive of healthy social life, not to say of democracy itself. This, in fact, is one reason for the attraction of the poor to Pentecostalism, in that the poorer neighbourhoods are the most ravaged by urban unrest. Resistance to the perpetrators of urban crime (in particular that associated with the drug culture) requires, however, considerable courage. In effecting their resistance, the appeal to a superior spiritual power becomes for Pentecostals a crucial and effective weapon, displayed amongst other things in the ritual of exorcism.

also of b other

It is necessary, finally, to take into account the cumulative effects of numerous changed lives, in so far as these are generative of social as well as (modest) economic capital. In terms of civil society, therefore, the positive effects of Pentecostal behaviour may well be clearer than at the level of State – the latter being off-limits for the greater number, if by no means all, Pentecostals. Freston is, however, cautious at this point: '[c]ivil society can also be uncivil' (2001: 298), i.e. generative of negative rather than positive consequences. The balance between voluntarism and fissiparousness on the one hand and repressive internal organisation, corporate interests and triumphalism on the other is finely poised (the scales can slip in either direction). A negative tilt can, moreover, end in scandal on a large scale, not least in connection with the media.

Repressive w/jara-zation

Freston's meticulous analyses underline a further point: it is crucial once again to recall the hugely varied political situations within Latin America, and within this the different alliances (or lack of these) of Church and State that have emerged in different parts of the continent. The delicate counterpoint between Protestant (including Pentecostals) and Catholic has to be worked out differently in different places. The particular niches which present themselves for Pentecostal action may, in consequence, lead in one place to one solution and in another to something entirely different (think of Peru, Chile, Brazil and Guatemala). Add to these the differences observed by Ireland at the micro level and the sheer complexity of the data becomes increasingly apparent. Patterns do indeed emerge from these accumulations of scholarship (it is the task of sociology to discern them), but

different scenarios

few universally applicable generalisations. The latter, however tempting, should be resisted.

THE SOCIOLOGICAL RESPONSE

Bearing such detail in mind, it is hardly surprising that the sociological commentators are far from unanimous. One point, however, is abundantly clear: despite an initial lack of attention, an enormous amount of work is now being done in the field with the effect that academic bibliographies are growing almost as fast as the Pentecostal churches.[9] Such work, however, is not confined to Pentecostalism but covers the whole range of religious activity in the region, not least the possession cults or spiritism, up to now mentioned only in passing. It is important, however, to note this aspect of Latin American and more especially Brazilian life, in that the expressions of Afro-Brazilian religion provide a significant link with a principal theme of the following chapter – that is the capacity of African religions to *export* themselves to different parts of the world, and not least to Latin America and the Caribbean. Candomblé is the clearest example of this tendency, with its origins in Nigerian Yoruba religion; Umbanda draws from a similar tradition but has its roots in Rio de Janeiro in the early twentieth century rather than in Africa itself.[10]

The major theme of this section, however, lies elsewhere. Its aim is to look again at the theoretical approaches (both European and American) outlined in previous chapters in order to 'measure' each of them against the material presented in this one. How well, in other words, can they cope with the data that is emerging from a different part of the world?

Chapter One set out a number of variations on the secularisation thesis. Bruce, following Wilson, was the principal exponent of the most rigorous of these approaches. Interestingly, in a developed parenthesis within *Religion in the Modern World*, Bruce

---

Pfa response to social change
along with secularisation ??

pays attention to the Latin American material, using the data to endorse, rather than critique, the secularisation thesis (1996: 113–25). His argument draws directly from Martin's *Tongues of Fire* in that it reinforces the connections between Methodism and Pentecostalism. Latin American Pentecostals, like British Methodists some two hundred years earlier, are experiencing rapid social change, not least the movement of large numbers of people from rural areas to the cities – a translation which brings with it a profound sense of rootlessness. It is in precisely this kind of situation that new forms of religion can gain a purchase, the more so for populations already accepting of the supernatural. Religion, in other words, has a specific (entirely understandable) job to do for particular kinds of people in conditions of accelerated social change.

It follows that the secularisation theory remains intact despite the rapid development of Pentecostalism in Latin America. The challenge to the thesis itself, according to Bruce, would only occur if previously secular populations were attracted in significant numbers to a religious revival. In a very narrow sense, and keeping the parameters of the secularisation thesis firmly in place (i.e. that it applies only to modern democratic societies), this is indeed plausible. Rather more problematic, however, is the realisation that it was precisely an over-preoccupation with secularisation conceptualised in these terms that blinded sociologists to what was happening in Latin America: quite simply they did not see and would not accept what theory forbade. Martin puts this as follows:

> The power of the ruling paradigms came home to me most forcibly on a bus full of Western academics in Guatamala. When told that 66 percent of the population was Catholic they asked no questions about where the rest might be, even though the answer shouted at them from texts on huts in remote El Petén, storehouse churches called 'Prince of Peace,' and buses announcing 'Jesus is coming'. (Martin 2001b: 27)

It is this kind of attitude that explains at least in part the heavily ideological critique of *Tongues of Fire* when it was first published.

Martin himself has constructed a rather different version of the secularisation theory, one that permits, indeed encourages, the possibility of different outcomes in different places (in Europe and in the United States for example). *Tongues of Fire* (1990) simply extends this process in that it maps the Latin American case in the terms set out in Martin's earlier *General Theory of Secularization* (1978), the former becoming in many ways the missing chapter in the latter. More specifically it creates a hybrid case bringing together both Anglo-Saxon and Latin variants, a synthesis which emphasises amongst other things the continuing possibility of religious change.[11]

In the more nuanced sense of secularisation offered by Martin, there is therefore a much more convincing fit between theory and data. The notion of vicariousness, in contrast – in the sense that I advanced this in *Religion in Modern Europe* – looks even more out of place in this chapter than it did with reference to the United States. Latin American Pentecostalists are not looking for institutions to carry a memory on their behalf. Quite the contrary, in fact: they are consciously and explicitly making a new start in churches that are essentially participatory, a point that will resonate even more strongly with reference to an African case study described in Chapter Four (Meyer 1998). The non-exportability of the vicariousness thesis can, however, be qualified a little. Given the European origins of the Catholic Church in Latin America, there is at least the possibility that vicariousness might work in a Catholic (with its large number of nominal believers) as opposed to a Pentecostal context. Ironically, it is precisely in this situation – that of unchurched and primarily Catholic religiosity – that Pentecostalism is gaining ground the fastest.

There are, finally, clear echoes of Callum Brown's thesis concerning the crucial role of women as carriers of religious culture; so much is common to both European and Latin American

experience. There is little sign, however, that this role is either
diminishing or altering radically in Latin America as Brown
claims to be the case in modern Britain. Entirely the opposite
in fact as Latin American women find solutions to their
dilemmas in the mutual support of the Pentecostal community
and, even more profoundly, in its transformative effect on the
traditional behaviour of men, who maintain none the less
the headship roles. Such ambiguity profoundly disconcerts the
Western feminist. Bernice Martin (2001) takes the argument
further still: feminist perspectives (rather like the traditional
versions of secularisation) were not only mistaken, they were
themselves part of the problem in so far as they blinded many
Western academics, though not the observers *sur place*
(anthropologists and missiologists), to much of what was
happening in Pentecostal communities. More specifically, the
feminist preoccupation with the oppression within both religion
and the family effectively blanked out the crucial and continuing
role of women in both spheres, through which a form of
liberation was indeed achieved but in ways undervalued by the
Western observer.

So much for the different versions of secularisation theory,
some of which 'do better' than others. Chapter Two introduced
the American alternative: rational choice theory. Can this help
us to a better understanding of the Latin American material?
There is, first of all, constant reference in the literature to the
increasing evidence of religious 'competition' in Latin America
(Levine 1995). Such competition is more apparent in the cities
than in rural areas, but exists in most, if not all, parts of the
region. Pentecostal congregations are not only springing up in
their thousands, but are recruiting actively, not to say aggressively,
for members. This, surely, is evidence of a religious market – a
term that is used with increasing frequency – with all the
implications that follow.

Given this situation it is surprising that the rational choice
theorists have come somewhat late, if at all, to the Latin

---

religious marketing

American field.[12] A notable exception can be found, however, in the work of Anthony Gill, who draws on RCT in his studies of Catholic policy-making in Latin America (Gill 1998, 1999). More specifically, Gill uses RCT to explain the decisions of some Catholic churches in the region in favour of an 'option for the poor', despite their 'traditional' stance as the ally of economic and political elites. The argument can be summarised as follows. RCT concentrates on the balance between incentives and costs. Using this Gill sets out the combination of factors that in his view will provide sufficient incentives for the Church to opt in favour of the poor, thus overcoming the costs of abandoning an alternative, and familiar policy. More specifically, in those places where the Catholic Church faces competition in the recruitment of believers – and especially from socialist and Protestant alternatives – the Catholic authorities will oppose authoritarian regimes in order to maintain credibility with the poor. It is clear that the presence of emergent Pentecostal movements becomes a crucial (if by no means the only) variable in this process as the Catholic Church looks for support among the poor. Gill exemplifies his theory with reference to the very different stances of the Catholic Church in Chile and Argentina. In the former case where there is a noticeable presence of both socialist and evangelical movements, the Pinochet regime has been heavily criticised. In the latter, where the alternatives are far less developed, the traditional accommodation between Church and State to a large extent continues.

The approach offers an unusual (in the sense that it is concerned with the choices made by churches rather than the choices made by believers) application of rational choice theory to the understanding of Latin American religion. The material, however, is extensive; together with a series of comments and criticisms, it is usefully gathered together on a website by Professor Gill himself.[13] Interestingly, in their more recent work, Finke and Stark (forthcoming) are beginning to draw on Gill's analyses as they review the possible applications of RCT outside the United States. The question of time-lag is crucial to their argument: in Latin America (as indeed was the case in the United States) religious growth follows deregulation but *not* immediately, a point with obvious resonance as we return once again to the European case.

LESSONS FOR EUROPE

What, then, are the lessons for Europe? The first, surely, is that things can and do change and often in very unexpected directions. The second point follows from this. Will they, *given sufficient time*, change in modern Europe and will they change in a similar direction? And if not, why not? Such questions must be kept apart from the associated value judgements, though the latter undoubtedly exist. There are bound to be those that envisage, and indeed pray for, revival in Europe almost exactly along the lines that it has occurred in Latin America. There are others, no doubt, who feel that a certain growth in levels of religious activity may well be desirable in Europe, but not quite in the way that has attracted so many Latin Americans in recent decades. It is precisely these questions that will be engaged in Chapter Six.

In the meantime, one thing is pretty certain: so far it hasn't happened. There are, of course, examples of both evangelical and Pentecostal growth in Europe, both inside and outside the historic churches. This is an area of church life that, relatively speaking, flourishes in a part of the world where the overall indicators are low. There are, moreover, interesting illustrations of Pentecostal growth on the fringes of the continent – where the institutional Church is at its weakest. Cucchiari's study of a Pentecostal community in Sicily provides an excellent illustration – all the more interesting given the evident ability of Sicilian Pentecostalism to confront the traditional, seemingly implacable patterns of Sicilian family life (Cucchiari 1988, 1991). The

---

P. in Sicily!

affinity between Pentecostalism and the gypsy populations of south, central and east Europe has also caught the attention of researchers, a phenomenon also discovered in Sweden (Skog 2001). Sweden, finally, is the rather surprising home of a different kind of Pentecostal community: the Livets Ord mega-church in Uppsala. Livets Ord (Word of Life) embodies a form of Pentecostalism that appeals to a relatively affluent section of the Swedish population. Its reference points lie in the Southern United States and its mission further East (not least the Soviet Union) – not, *explicitly not*, in the historic deposits of Scandinavian Lutheranism (Coleman 2000).[14]

By and large, however, we must conclude that the principal question facing us at this point is to explain why the very significant growth in Pentecostalism that can be seen in Latin America has not for the most part occurred in Latin Europe (or indeed anywhere else in the continent). In other words, there is nothing in Europe that could be described as a widespread and popular Pentecostal movement, involving significant sections of the population with a corresponding change in life-style. Why not?

One way of tackling this question is to think comparatively, i.e. to identify spaces for Pentecostalism in Latin America that are not, or not yet, present in Europe. We have already seen that Latin American patterns of religion derive historically from the Latin variant in Europe. On this side of the Atlantic, this took the form of a relatively well-disciplined Catholic monopoly on one side, confronted (at times aggressively) by an anti-clerical secularism on the other. Each encouraged the other and in some parts of Europe, notably nineteenth- and early twentieth-century France, the clash between Catholic Church and secular State became the defining feature of political life. It is equally clear, however, that a similar conflict despite significant attempts never quite took hold in Latin America. We need to appreciate why.

Material (both historical and current) from the Latin American context indicates a marked lack of control on both sides of the

Europe: The Exceptional Case

Why no-where else?

no Catholic church - state conflict in Latin Am.
as in Europe to promote secularism

equation. Birman and Pereira Leite, for example, consider *throughout*
the Brazilian Catholic Church in these terms – using an argument that can be constructed both positively and negatively. On *society*
the positive side, the Catholic Church is seen as tolerant and
welcoming, drawing into itself the varied currents of Brazilian
life, not least the possession cults that came, directly or indirectly, *in Lat. A*
from Africa. Cordiality, moreover, is a valued characteristic
which endorses the claim of the Catholic Church to be the *so/a*
national Church of Brazil. The downside, however, is relatively *less*
weak doctrinal control, manifested in the myriad forms of *controlled*
popular religion (a whole pantheon of saints and demons) that
continue to exist inside as well as outside the official Church. *R C ch.*
Boundary maintenance, dogmatic or otherwise, is well-nigh *no*
impossible (Birman and Pereira Leite 2000: 271–3). *'boundary'*

This, however, is only half the story. The other half can be *is-*
found in the failure of the secular elite, just as much as the *maintain-ance'*
Catholic hierarchy, to exert an equivalent discipline on significant
sections of the population. Secularism undoubtedly exists but it
remains the preserve of the elite, failing to penetrate the mass of
the population (Martin 2001). In consequence, the division
of society over the question of religion as such (epitomised in
the French case) simply did not occur in Brazil – or indeed *popular*
in most of Latin America, with the partial exception of Euro- *religiosity*
peanised Uruguay. Either way, it is the resistant popular religiosity *always*
of the mass of the population which becomes the key explanation *prevailed*
for the very different scenario. Such religiosity becomes, at one
and the same time, a highly fertile seedbed for Pentecostalism and
the effective limit to hierarchical control.

One final question remains: might the same thing happen in
Europe, if not immediately, then at least in the longer term? At
this point the argument in this chapter rejoins that presented in
the previous one – i.e. the case study of the United States. In
that chapter, I argued strongly against the artificial adoption of
North American answers to European questions. In my view, it
is not possible to create the kind of market found in the United

States within the European context and probably foolish to try. Other scenarios might, however, be possible. For example, European 'spaces', previously occupied by hegemonic national churches (not to mention their secular alter-egos), could gradually open up to permit new forms of religion. We have already seen that this is happening round the edges of the continent, whether these be defined geographically (in Sicily, for example) or socially (the gypsy populations). Could the process become more widespread?

Precisely this point has already been made by Martin. I first used the following quotation in a chapter in *Religion in Modern Europe* (in other words looking at Europe from the inside). Looked at from the outside (and in the first instance from Latin America), it seems even more apposite:

> Initially, about a quarter of a century ago, I asked myself why the voluntary denominations of Anglo-American culture had not taken off in Latin America as they had in the U.S.A., and concluded that Latin America must be too similar to Latin Europe for that to happen. But now I am inclined to reverse the question and ask why the burgeoning denominations of Latin America have not taken off in Latin Europe . . . There are new spaces being cleared in which a competitive denominational culture can flourish. (1996: 41; citation taken from the English original)

The essence of Martin's approach lies in the observation that the factors that encouraged European secularisation in the first place – a fortress Catholicism, buttressed by political power, and opposed by militant secularity – are themselves beginning to erode. There is no reason, therefore, why the voluntary denominationalism of the New World should not find a place in the Old, alongside if not replacing a weakened Catholic Church. And if that is true in Latin Europe, how much more spectacular are the spaces in much of the former communist world, which, quite clearly, are attracting sustained attention from the evangelical

possibilities of P. in old communist world?

constituency all over the West, to the dismay at times of the
historic churches. This reversal of the 'normal' flows will become
a primary theme in subsequent chapters — most immediately
with reference to the African case.

Chapter Four

AFRICAN INITIATIVES:
AN ALTERNATIVE VIEW OF
GLOBAL RELIGION

Given the size and diversity of modern Africa, this chapter must be even more selective than the others. Chapter Three took as its principal theme the dramatic growth of Pentecostalism in many parts of Latin America and attempted to explain why the same phenomenon had not (so far at least) occurred in Europe. Exactly the same could be done for sub-Saharan Africa, a fact which illustrates the truly global nature of Pentecostalism at the start of the twenty-first century. For the African chapter, I have, however, chosen a different emphasis – namely the capacity of African people to export their religious life to many parts of the modern world, and not least in recent years to Europe. The two chapters overlap in so far as the churches of the newly-arrived African congregations are very often, though not always, Pentecostal in nature, but the point of departure is differently conceived.

The impact of African forms of religion in various parts of Europe is a relatively new field of enquiry; it is, however, one that fits the theme of these lectures very precisely. Quite apart from this, it is a subject which many Europeans find provocative in so far as it questions many of their most deep-seated assumptions. Or to put the same point more sharply, the relationship between Europe and Africa is assumed to operate in a particular

84

Pentacostalism & other forms from Africa to Europe

direction: its apparent reversal is correspondingly disturbing. Ter Haar, for example, underlines the self-understanding of Ghanaian communities in The Netherlands, arguably one of the most secular countries of Western Europe. They see themselves as missionaries in a secular continent. Drawing on the Old Testament image of 'dry bones', members of these churches construct Europe as a spiritual desert to which they are called as evangelists, a fact that is not always appreciated by the host society.

> The reversal of responsibilities implied in this attitude drastically overturns the traditional relations between Africans and Europeans. It is in sharp contrast with the conventional view of existing north-south relations, often equated with black-white relations, and hardly conforms to the marginal position of the majority of Africans in Europe. On the European side, this reversal of roles appears difficult to appreciate as it does not comply with the stereotypes often attached to Africa. Africans are traditionally represented as on the receiving end and Europe on the giving end of a relationship characterised by unequal transfer. (Ter Haar 1998a: 168)

But this is to anticipate the conclusion of the chapter too soon. In order to appreciate the impact of this kind of role reversal, it is necessary to put in place the various layers of African religion from which such 'missionaries' come and the crucial role of Europeans in Africa's Christianisation process. One way of tackling this question is, at least in part, to follow the themes introduced in the *Journal of Religion in Africa* as these are set out in the retrospective reflections, both chronological and thematic, of its retiring editor (Hastings 2000). Such reflections operate as a *fil conducteur* through the complexities that are inevitable in even the shortest summary of the religious field in this enormous and diverse continent. They, like African religion itself, are multi-layered. Not only do they furnish a set of themes by which to organise the material, they provide in addition comment on the associated literature.

---

leaving out Islam

Before embarking on this venture, two preliminary points are important. The first is to stress that the chapter concentrates almost entirely on sub-Saharan Africa, i.e. on the parts of Africa influenced by Christianity rather than Islam. The latter, of course, is of vital importance in order to understand the continent as a whole, but not everything can be included here. With this in mind the emphasis will inevitably fall on Anglophone rather than Francophone Africa and will leave on one side the issue of Christian-Islamic relations despite their growing importance in geo-political debate. The second point is rather different and emerges directly from the fact that both the research for this chapter and its preliminary draft were undertaken in the University of Uppsala, Sweden, the home base of the scholar and pastor Bengt Sundkler whose career as an Africanist lasted more than half a century. His first major book *Bantu Prophets in South Africa* was published in 1948, the last volume (well over 1000 pages) was published posthumously (with the help of Christopher Steed) in 2000. An obvious consequence of Sundkler's work is the admirable collection of material on African religion in the libraries of his home university, something for which I was extremely grateful, if at times rather overwhelmed by the sheer volume of what was available. This seems an appropriate place to acknowledge the unique contribution of Sundkler to the field of African studies.

THE AFRICAN CONTEXT

Two somewhat contradictory features of modern Africa need underlining at the outset. The first concerns the demographic shift in world Christianity, the second the economic collapse in most, if not quite in all, of the African continent. A developed discussion of the latter is, quite clearly, beyond the remit of the present chapter, though its influence will resonate at a number of places in the text – not least as a push factor in encouraging

Africans to move elsewhere in the world, including Europe. At this point, however, a rather different consideration requires attention: that is the effects of economic uncertainty on African scholarship itself, a fact widely recognised by those working in the field. Hastings, for example, emphasises the seriousness of the economic situation for the study of African Christianity particularly in the later post-war decades:

> That brings us to the 1980s, the nadir of our history. What exactly happened? The first and most decisive cause was, unquestionably, the rundown of African universities north of the Zambezi: the erosion of salaries, the book famine, the disappearance of periodicals . . . University decline was, of course, within a context of wider political unrest and economic stagnation, all greatly inhibiting the work of research. In the 1960s one took it for granted that the generation of Ajayi and Ayadele would be followed and excelled by a burgeoning academic army all across Africa. It never happened. (Hastings 2000: 37)

There has been a marked recovery in the sub-discipline in the 1990s but the difficulties of African universities north of the Zambezi remain acute.

The need for African Christian studies has, however, never been greater. Walls (1996) emphasises two aspects of this work: first the continuing need to document the specifically African story, but second to realise that the African narrative has become increasingly a pivotal chapter in the history of Christianity itself. To illustrate this point, Walls used his introductory paper at a Conference of Christianity in Africa in the 1990s[1] to compare the state of affairs in Africa in the 1990s with that evoked at an earlier conference in Edinburgh: the World Missionary Conference of 1910.[2] The latter divided the world into the 'missionised' and the 'non-missionised' areas. The fully missionised included Europe, North America, Australia and New Zealand. The 'not yet fully missionised' was essentially everyone else, not least the whole of Africa (apart from a small section of South Africa). Interestingly nothing at all was said about Latin America (in order it seems to avoid dividing the conference delegates). Asia, moreover, was the prime focus of missionary attention, rather than Africa.

Since 1910 the demography of world Christianity has altered dramatically. Active Christianity in 'fully-missionised' West Europe has manifestly receded, whereas large sections of the 'not fully missionised' globe have become centres of Christian vitality – those largely which are covered by the case studies described in these chapters. And none more so than Africa itself where the indices of both practice and belief (never mind the absolute numbers) are some of the highest in the world (Barrett 1982, Barrett *et al.* 2001). Hence the crucial importance of the African story to the evolution of Christianity as a whole. An obvious, rather more domestic illustration of the same metamorphosis can be seen in the shifting nature of the Lambeth Conference (the decennial meeting of Bishops of the Anglican Communion convened by the Archbishop of Canterbury). From something dominated by the English (and English ways of doing things), it has become increasingly global in its reach and includes a crucial African presence. The emergence of markedly different and at times conflicting agendas are part and parcel of the same process. Undoubtedly difficult to manage from the point of view of the conference organisers, such agendas caused in 1998 even greater consternation amongst the secular journalists.

LAYERS OF AFRICAN RELIGION

The beginnings

The long-term movement of both people and ideas from Europe to all parts of the African continent is of crucial significance in understanding the multiplicity of religious layers that exist in modern Africa. Such movement is not, however, the starting point. That is to be found in Africa itself, first in the presence of the Christian Church considerably *before* it existed in most parts of Europe and second in the traditional religions of Africa. More specifically, in the early centuries of the Christian era, there were important Christian deposits both in the Mediterranean coastlands (and their hinterlands) and in the Horn of Africa. Indeed the emergence of Europe as a Christian entity (that described in Chapter One) comes later and, as a process, is inseparable from the spread of Islam in the seventh and eighth centuries. With the advance of Islam, the unity of the Mediterranean world was shattered once and for all, out of which emerged three distinct civilisations (indeed three calendars): that of Rome, Byzantium and Islam.

The latter overran the great majority of the Christian churches in North Africa with the exception of the Coptic Church in Egypt, a presence which then spread southward up the Nile valley into the land of Nubia, leading in 710 to a Nubian Christian state. Christianity survived in Nubia until the fifteenth century when it too succumbed to persistent Islamification. In Ethiopia, in contrast, Christianity not only came earlier (the fourth century) but survived. Ethiopian Christianity, moreover, possessed unique features, not least an identity which linked the Jewish background of the early Church with specifically African elements. It acquired, in consequence, considerable symbolic importance as a distinctively African Church with its own faith and its own traditions – features which were to resonate strongly in the nineteenth and twentieth centuries. Many African religious movements have adopted the name Ethiopian to signify an African Christianity independent from Western domination.

Given the exponential growth of Christianity (as indeed of Islam) in the twentieth century, what has happened to the traditional religions of Africa that existed before the coming of Europeans to most parts of the continent? Walls (1996) argues that such religions continue within Christianity itself – the distinctive nature of African Christianity cannot in fact be understood without reference to what has gone before. There are, following Walls, more continuities than discontinuities, in the fact, for example, that the Christian God in Africa has a vernacular name and in the application of the Christian tradition to already existing maps of the universe. The latter point is crucial:

> It is true, as we shall see, that the relationships between the components of those maps – God, local divinities, ancestors, objects of power – have changed, and changed radically, as a result of the Christian impact; but as components in understanding the world and society they remain in one guise or another. In order to have an effect in Africa, the Christian tradition has thus had to be applied to these pre-existing components; it has been placed on the available maps of the universe, and interpreted within existing categories. (Walls 1996: 5)

The argument about continuities should not, of course, be taken too far. Many changes have occurred – the world view has been re-ordered and new elements have been introduced – but for some commentators the persistence of the older components remains paramount, prompting the specificity of African theology as well as African religion.[3] Walls, for example, suggests that much of the distinctiveness of African theology lies in the manner in which it formalises the syntheses produced by the lives of countless African Christians as they affirm, deny, suppress, redirect and reinterpret the traditional forms of African religion in light of Christian teaching (1996: 14).

Others are less sure. Indeed the debate regarding continuity and discontinuity becomes a pervasive theme in the literature as a whole and will resonate repeatedly. With respect to the coming of Christianity, Maxwell, for instance, stresses rupture as much as continuity in both theology and behaviour: 'Christianity brought many new and powerful ideas: sin and hell, judgement and redemption. It introduced Africans to Christ and Mary, who . . .

The distinctiveness
of African theology

demanded unwavering devotion' (Maxwell 2001: 8). In terms of behaviour, the most dramatic disjuncture of all, following Maxwell, lies with African women, in, for example, the role of the celibate nun – an entirely new idea.

European influences – the missionary centuries

One thing is abundantly clear: the influence of Europe and Europeans has been decisive for the evolution of Christianity in Africa. In Sundkler's and Steed's massive overview, for example, roughly forty pages describe the first 1500 years (pages which are used in addition to set out a range of seminal themes); the remaining 1000 deal with the colonial story and its aftermath.

The first to arrive (in the late fifteenth century) were the Portuguese, significant for a number of reasons. First Portuguese troops (newly enthused by the *Reconquista* at home) helped the Ethiopians to repulse a fierce Muslim attack in the 1540s, a crucial event in the survival of the Ethiopian Church. Further south, coastal communities emerged in Angola and Mozambique as the result of settlement, trade and intermarriage. More enduring and more profoundly Christian, however, was the elective monarchy of Mbanza Kongo (at the mouth of the Congo) established in the early sixteenth century, an impressive venture eventually undermined by the insensitivities of the Europeans, despite the genuine attempts by the Africans to incorporate Lusitanian culture. Finally it is important to note the role of the Portuguese in the emergent slave trade on both sides of the Atlantic (North and South), the beginnings of African emigrations to the new world.

As the dominance of the Portuguese gradually diminished, their place was taken in the seventeenth and eighteenth centuries by Northern Europe's Protestant states – notably the Dutch (in South Africa) and the British, the latter heavily involved in both the slave trade itself and in the struggles to bring this to an end. The founding of the free colonies of Sierra Leone and Liberia are central to this history, themselves embodying a new concept: the notion of an African Christian civilisation free from slavery, led by Africans, but modelled first and foremost on the Protestant west.

It was, however, in the 'long nineteenth century' that the missionary enterprise became the dominant theme. The story is complex and multi-layered, unsurprisingly given the size and diversity of the African continent. It can, moreover, be told from different points of view. Sundkler, for example, indicates two quite different 'maps' that can be drawn to describe and to explain the Christianisation process that took place in nineteenth-century Africa. The first is the 'official' missionary map, locating the centres (or chains of centres) of a well-defined missionary programme. The materials required to furnish this history are to be found in the histories of the missionary societies and their mission fields and in the biographies (sometimes hagiographies) of the missionaries themselves. Beneath such schemes, however, can be found a different, and in some ways more penetrating map: one that concentrates on the movements and migrations of the African populations themselves and their own role in spreading the gospel. It is to this map that Sundkler (and indeed others) give precedence. 'In the following pages, the reader will meet an emphasis on vast and dramatic changes, in and through the adversities and opportunities, with uprooted refugee – groups and individuals – in "the spreading chaos of the interior plains", prepared to face and join the new religion' (Sundkler and Steed 2000: 82). The refugee motif becomes in fact a primary theme of the book as a whole.[4] The crucial moments arrive, however, at the points of intersection between the two maps, when a major transition (or conversion) takes place from traditional ways of living to the new faith.

Sundkler's following chapters tell this rich and varied story, in which distinctive patterns emerge – both regional and social. The regional pattern, first of all, emphasises the contrasting characteristics of the different parts of Africa – in each time

---

Europe: The Exceptional Case

period, Sundkler follows the same 'route', moving from the North to the West, to the South and then the East. Cross-cutting the regions (with important exceptions and variations), however, are the key social categories: the kings and chiefs, the young men, and the slaves and other socially marginalised groups. Consonant with his stress on the second of the two 'maps' described above, Sundkler argues that the first to join the new Church were, very often, the aliens, the foreigners and the uprooted. The African Church in the nineteenth century was moreover very largely a youth movement. It was the young men who had least to lose and most to gain as they struck out; herein lay the core of mobility and movement, characteristic of both African society and African religion.[5]

Finally even *within* the broad periodisation of Sundkler's story as a whole – the long nineteenth century (1787–1919), the colonial experience (1920–59) and independent Africa (1960–92) – there are important shifts in emphasis. It is, for example, in the last quarter of the nineteenth century that the real 'European scramble' for power and empire takes place; policies that took geo-political shape after the Congress of Berlin in 1885 as Europe's leading statesmen carved the African continent into pieces largely for their own consumption, a crucial moment in European as well as African history. Christian missions were both an essential part of this process (defending or claiming particular territories) and critical of it (soundly condemning, for example, the worst excesses of economic exploitation in the Belgian Congo). The European scrambles were, moreover, multifaceted embodying economic and political as well as religious transformations. They were part, in fact, of an immense metamorphosis in the life of Africa, as the continent gradually took its place in the global capitalist economy. The role of Christianity (and indeed of Islam) as catalysts in this globalising process became the focus of a much discussed article published in 1971 (Horton 1971).[6] In this, Horton argues that Christianity (like Islam) has particular resonance as a world faith, stimulating

---

African Initiatives

Globalising influence of Christianity & Islam

and accelerating shifts that were in the air anyway; offering, in other words, the intellectual and conceptual resources to cope with the immensities of change, as the microcosm gradually turned into the macrocosm and Africa became part of the emergent world order.

Horton's analysis remains controversial. Peel, for example, re-emphasises the crucial role of both the missionaries and their message and the specificities of the context, including the associated power structures, in which the missionary encounters take place (Peel 2000: 4). But either way the European occupation of Africa, including its religious dimensions, was decisive. Its effects were multiple and irreversible as old authorities (political and religious) either disappeared altogether or were vastly reduced. This was the moment when Europeans imposed on Africans, either directly or indirectly, their languages, their systems of education and administration, their political traditions, a European literary culture, modern forms of transport and – most decisive of all – a system of tax (Hastings 1994: 403). An immediate effect of the latter and its implications for economic life (as indeed of the European influence as a whole) was the manifest need for literacy, and hence education. This in turn stimulated a huge demand for schools, including mission schools. The need for education and the contrasting policies of the British and the French in this field, becomes, in consequence, an increasingly important aspect of the story as the nineteenth century gives way to the twentieth. It cannot be covered in detail in this chapter, but resonates strongly in both Sundkler's and Hasting's accounts of the later period.

One final remark concludes this section; it relates very immediately to the broader theme of these lectures and concerns the retrospective views of many Europeans with respect to the missionary enterprise (both in Africa and elsewhere). In the post-war decades (most notably in the 1960s), such enterprise has had a bad press in Europe; it has been seen primarily as a form of cultural oppression profoundly damaging to 'native' beliefs and civilisations. Such critiques have been led by the secular-liberal lobby, a group already critical of Christianity in its European context. Exactly the same personnel seem paradoxically unaware, however, that in many ways they are themselves participating in a similar enterprise: effectively they are 'exporting' secularisation, just as their forebears exported Christianity. But with one difference. For this group, the export of secularisation remains largely unquestioned in so far as many Europeans assume that as the world modernised, it would *necessarily* secularise. In contrast the earlier product, Christian mission, was (and still is) repeatedly censured.

There are, of course, two sides to the debate about mission. In some ways the secular liberals are right — African beliefs and cultures were indeed disturbed if not destroyed altogether. Such critics, however, frequently underestimate both the sheer cost of mission in terms of the individuals involved,[7] and — rather differently — the significance of the religious encounter in the lives of the recipients (a moment of deciding between old ways and new). Bearing these complexities in mind, Peel's *Religious Encounter and the Making of the Yoruba* (2000) should become required reading for all those interested in mission.

African Independent Churches

It is time now to turn to a rather different strand in the history of African Christianity: the multiplicity of churches founded by 'black African for black African' and 'devoted to the well-being, salvation and liberation of African people' (Daneel 1998: 22). Just how different this strand is, however, raises once again the issue of continuity and discontinuity: the line between mission churches and African Independent Churches (AICs) is not always as sharp as is sometimes imagined. Quite clearly the success of the mission churches depended to a large extent on labour migrants, refugees, African evangelists and catechists (a point already established); AICs in their turn are fed more than some commentators appreciate by currents from outside Africa (not least by the descendants of the slave population in the United States). The system is by no means closed.

The emphasis, however, *is* different. Precedents for independency can be found in the eighteenth century, but the majority of AICs date from the early twentieth century as a sense of pan-Africanism emerged as a significant force, and particularly in South Africa. They vary in size from the very small to movements embracing millions of adherents. Most, it is important to remember, are distinctively Christian and form part of the mainstream of Christian activity in Africa; these are by no means marginal or sectarian movements. Among the larger groups can be found the following: the *amaNazareta* of Isaiah Shembe and the Zion Christian Church of Engenas Lekganyane, both in South Africa; Samuel Mutendi's Zion Christian Church and Johane Maranke's African Apostolic Church in Zimbabwe; Alice Lenshina's Lumpa Church in Zambia; Simon Kimbangu's Church of Jesus Christ in Zaire (the largest of all); and finally the Cherubim and Seraphim Church and the Church of the Lord (Aladura) in Nigeria.

Continuing to follow Daneel (1998), three broad types can be distinguished in the literature. The first includes the Ethiopian type or non-prophetic church movements which emerge as a reaction to the white-led mission churches, though in other respects are very like them. It is these churches, moreover, that embody an 'Ethiopian' or distinctively African ideology – i.e. one that is free from European influence. The second or spirit-type place much greater emphasis on the work of the Holy Spirit, displayed in charismatic forms of worship and prophetic gifts including healing and various forms of exorcism. Daneel includes in this category all Zionists and a wide range of Apostolic churches. Finally there are the Messianic churches (a more controversial category), in which the founder-leader of the church or movement becomes much more central (as a miracle worker or resistance figure, for example), displacing in some

Ethiopian / Zionist - apostolic / Messianic

senses the centrality of Christ. The controversy surrounds the degree to which the leader obscures the salvific work of Christ.

Hastings, however, mitigates these distinctions, feeling that they are easily overstated (Hastings 1994: 501, 533). He prefers instead to refer to an Ethiopian end and a prophetic end to the spectrum, each of which appealed to rather different people – *on the whole* the former to a new elite of clergy and laity (irritated by European control) and the latter to the very poor (opting out of a white-dominated secular world and into a more religious one). Such distinctions form part of a wider discussion of the causes and motivations of independency. This was first of all a Protestant movement, part in fact of the naturally fissiparous nature of Protestantism, much of which had become by this time a somewhat cerebral form of faith out of touch with the biblical context (of healing and miracles etc.). With this in mind, three more specific factors should also be taken into account. The first derives from the colonial and racial nature not only of society, but of the Church itself, which consistently marginalised the African in favour of even the most recently arrived European. The second factor picks up a point made earlier, that is the continuing influence of traditional African religion and culture within Christianity itself, a fact which resonated strongly with a biblical tradition: hence a 'sort of biblical-African alliance against the rather more rationalist, but also simply more rigidly denominationalist, missionary' (1994: 529), sufficient in many places to stimulate the prophetic side of the independent churches. Health and healing were central to the latter movement, reacting against Western medical practice on the one hand and aspects of traditional medicine (the fear of spiritual powers and life-threatening exorcism) on the other, a point strongly reinforced by Sundkler (2000: 677–9).

The final factor in explaining the growth of AICs lies in the sheer expansion of the Christian scene. In the early twentieth century, the mission churches could hardly keep up with what was happening, a situation in which the prophet emerged to

---

a Protestant independency
a biblical-African alliance v.
rational western mission & medicine

take on the missionary's task (precisely because of its importance). According to Hastings, the process was more one of conversion than of secession. In baptism, for example, it is indeed 'the continuity in experience rather than any discontinuity between mission and independency which requires recognition' (1994: 531). The difference lies more in the modes of preparation. Missionaries insisted on the thoroughness of this; independency in contrast came close to responding to the demand for instant baptism by generating prophetic baptisers. Whatever the case, the years between 1910 and 1940 saw a proliferation of conversion movements in many parts of Africa, partly driven by the rigidities of the missionary churches or, conversely, by their absence. Different patterns emerged in different places, but in significant parts of Africa (notably the South), independency became a crucially important part of the growing Church.

Not only did the AICs expand, so too did the scholarship related to this topic. Sundkler, for example, notes the number of studies devoted to such movements, many of which are brought together in Turner's magisterial bibliography (Turner 1977).[8] Rather more serious, however, is Sundkler's subsequent indictment: '[T]here is undeniably a certain tendency to romanticism in some of this literary activity. If Africa was to be "the Christian Continent" at all it must be so, not in any recognizable Western form, but preferably dressed in as surprising a garment as possible' (2000: 1033). Hasting's reflections regarding the *Journal of Religion in Africa* are rather similar. Emphasising first the evident 'fit' between the prevalent mood of the 1960s and 1970s (i.e. the early years of the journal) and the search for African initiatives, including AICs, Hastings was at times less happy about the quality. This varied from the truly excellent – work that was properly contextualised and historically/theologically informed – to studies which clearly displayed some of the 'romanticism' already pointed out by Sundkler. The 'industry' finally ran out of steam in the 1980s, an additional reason for the downturn of the fortunes of the journal in this decade (see above). Gradually, in a

a romantic vision → the 'industry' runs out of steam

tendency welcomed by Hastings, it was counter-balanced by a re-focusing of scholarly attention on the mission-founded churches of Africa. In order for both to be properly understood, the two aspects of African religion should be seen as complementary parts of a single whole, not simply in terms of schism.

Modern Pentecostalism

In terms of scholarship, Pentecostalism in Africa is differently placed. Compared on the one hand with the study of AICs in Africa, and on the other with the very extensive work devoted to Pentecostalism in Latin America, *relatively* little has been done in this increasingly significant field. There are, however, important beginnings – for example, the collection of case studies brought together in *New Dimensions in African Christianity* (Gifford 1992).[9]

In his introductory essay to this volume, Gifford pursues a series of questions: i.e. questions about numbers, about provenance (from which churches do the new Pentecostals come?), about typologies (to what extent are the traditional typologies still applicable?), about 'Africanness', about politics and finally about the connection between Pentecostal movements and Africa's economic collapse. Within this rather daunting list, it is worth pausing for a moment on 'Africanness' in that it raises the problematic distinction between new forms of Pentecostalism and more traditional forms of independency, parts of which have quite rightly been described as Pentecostal.

> In what way are these new churches a flowering of African Christianity? What attitude do these new pentecostal churches adopt towards African Culture? To what extent is this new African Christianity underpinned by an African metaphysic? What is the Western factor in this phenomenon? To what degree are Western missionaries involved? What role do Western literature, technology, media play? To what degree

African ? Pentacostalian

is the theology of these new movements Western? (Gifford 1992: 5)

Beneath such questions, the issue of continuity reappears once again and in a particularly complicated form. Harvey Cox (1996), for example, regards AICs as the African expression of worldwide Pentecostalism. In a later volume, Gifford (1998: 33) feels that this is a serious category mistake, underlining instead the markedly different nature of modern forms of Pentecostalism. Peel (2000), thirdly, offers a both/and rather than either/or solution for the Nigerian case. There are indeed striking differences between the two groups in 'style, idiom and emphasis', notably the Pentecostal stress on new beginnings and their anxiety to look out rather than back (emphasising above all their membership of a fast-growing and worldwide movement). 'Yet basically the born-agains and the Aladura share the same worldview, with its deep Yoruba (or Nigerian, or African) roots', an outlook which has both positive and negative features (2000: 314–5).

Martin (2001a) offers further clarification. Pentecostals, he argues, inhabit a niche between the AICs and the historic churches, rejecting both the Africanisation of the former and the political critique and commitment to inculturation of the latter. Pentecostals, in contrast, are essentially forward looking, shedding the ties that hold them back in their search for mobility, freedom and advancement. Their familial, economic and political attitudes follow from this, but take different forms in different places. An important aspect of Martin's synthesis echoes, however, a point made earlier: that is the *continuing* migrations and mobilities of African society, but this time to the megacities of late modernity, in which the Pentecostal community offers rootedness (in a voluntary community) to those for whom the ties of nation or ethnicity no longer resonate.

Martin's analysis is based on an overview of recent case studies, almost all of which date from the 1990s. Four of these have been brought together in a special issue of the *Journal of Religion in*

Europe: The Exceptional Case

forward-looking & trans-national

Africa.[10] Maxwell's editorial underlines the by now familiar points: the dramatic growth of African Pentecostalism in the last decades of the twentieth century, its vitality and the complexity of its effects on the traditional alignments of African Christianity. Within this framework, two of the studies pay particular attention to the mass media and their role in the life of Pentecostal communities.[11] For Hackett (1998) this is the major theme of her paper, but her argument also includes a strong emphasis on transnationalism and the flows of information across international boundaries. For Marshall-Fratani (1998) it is almost the other way round: transnationalism is the starting point, an idea that has particular resonance for Pentecostals as they seek identities beyond the nation state. With this in mind the connections between the global and the local (in this case Nigeria) become crucial to Marshall's argument, within which the media pay a central role – facilitating the circulation of images and narratives. Pentecostal people are, however, equally mobile. Nigerian evangelists, for example, preach at international conferences alongside Korean and Brazilians, whilst *international* ministries are maintained in different parts of an ever-growing Nigerian diaspora (including, interestingly, Manchester and London). The capacity of Pentecostalism to operate across borders becomes a pivotal theme (see below).

Meyer's work on Ghana, together with Maxwell's own on Zimbabwe, focuses on the relationship between Pentecostalism and modernity itself. Using material from a detailed ethnographic study of the Zimbabwe Assemblies of God, Africa (ZAOGA), Maxwell (1998, 1999) addresses two interrelated issues: the prosperity gospel itself and its links to the American bible belt. Both are controversial. Maxwell concludes that there is indeed contact between Zimbabwe and the United States in terms of theological justification for the accumulation of wealth, but that Southern African sources and local concerns are paramount for the members of ZAOGA, not least the need to establish ways of surviving in conditions of rapid economic

the Nigerian diaspora

the Zimbabwe Assemblies of God &
the American prosperity gospel

breaking with the past: remembering + forgetting

change. In so far as it succeeds in this aim, Pentecostalism in
Africa (just as in Latin America) fits well with both the values
and the institutions of modernity.

Meyer (1998, 1999) engages modernity in a different way,
examining the tension between 'making a complete break with
the past' (so often characteristic of Pentecostalism) and the cultural policies encouraged by the Ghanaian State. More
specifically Pentecostals oppose the re-assertions of tradition and
culture favoured by the post-colonial State,[12] preferring the glo-
balised and forward-looking character of Pentecostal religion
(exemplifying both Peel's and Martin's point very precisely). The
process, however, is complex: Meyer demonstrates, for example,
'how pentecostalism seeks a rupture from a "tradition" or "past"
which it has previously helped to construct, thereby engaging
in a dialectics of remembering and forgetting' (1998: 318).
Believers can only forget what they first 'construct' as the past;
the forgetting is achieved through deliverance. Meyer's analysis
goes further still. She demonstrates how believers cannot in fact
make a complete break with the past and turn once and for all
into 'free' and modern individuals. The success of Pentecostalism
resides precisely in its capacity to address this ambiguity.

It is interesting to reflect on Meyer's work in connection with
that of Hervieu-Léger introduced in Chapter One. For both the
idea of memory is central, i.e. that which links an individual to
a chain of generations and (in the African case) to a web of
kinship relationships. For Hervieu-Léger, religion is seen as part
and parcel of this process – indeed linking a believer to a specific
chain of memory becomes the defining feature of religion. For
Meyer, almost the reverse is true: for Ghanaian Pentecostals the
identity of the born again Christian resides not in memory as
such 'but in the rejection of all the links revealed by it' (1998:
339–40). The power of the past needs to be broken, not per-
petuated, a rupture which requires a powerful ritual and
explanatory discourse (supplied in this case by the distinctiveness
of Pentecostal worship and teaching).

What churches challenge the state?
— or dictators

CROSS-CUTTING THEMES

Going back once again to Hasting's article, the *fil conducteur* of this chapter, a new set of themes emerge in the *Journal* in the 1990s. In addition to Pentecostalism itself, Hastings lists the following: Church-State relationships, Christian-Islamic relationships, a renewed emphasis on missionary history and the AIC diaspora. It will be the last of these (indeed the African diaspora more generally) that preoccupies us in the following section, but before engaging this particularly pertinent theme, just a few words should be said about the other three.

Paul Gifford's contribution to the understanding of Church and State has been crucial (Gifford 1995, 1998). In *The Christian Churches and the Democratisation of Africa* (1995), Gifford brings together the papers from a prestigious conference held at the University of Leeds two years earlier. In this, he highlights the role of the churches in the democratisation process (especially the Catholic Church in the French-speaking parts of the continent), a role which surprised many Western observers in that (as ever) they were not prepared for it. Why not is the question that follows. Once again the dearth in African scholarship becomes a significant factor, but the predominantly secular anticipations of Europeans is, as ever, another. Nor should it be assumed that the churches necessarily act unanimously in the political sphere. Gifford distinguishes carefully between the mainline churches which for the most part challenge Africa's dictators, and the newer evangelical or Pentecostal churches which often provide support. The latter remark is, however, immediately qualified – endorsing a point already made in connection with Latin America. Paradoxically, evangelical or Pentecostal churches 'may in the long run do more for political reform than the mainline churches and any "liberation theology" ' (1995: 5), in that simply by existing the new churches are creating freer social space (an essential element in autonomous action), not least at the level of civil society.[13]

Africa, however, is a continent of change and in re-assessing the public role of Christianity in 1998, Gifford is forced to acknowledge the cataclysmic nature of events in both (Protestant) Liberia and (Catholic) Rwanda. It is hard to be comfortable about Christianity's role in either of these cases. Gifford's reaction is to use these profoundly negative experiences constructively: that is to scrutinise ever more closely the adequacy of the churches' (plural) response to the highly problematic situation in which they find themselves.

One way of doing this is to follow Hastings' advice and to return once again to the careful assessment of the missionary churches as a keystone of African religion. The geo-political circumstances of the 1990s, both inside and outside Africa, are however very different from those prior to 1960, when the shift towards AICs (quite rightly) typified the mood. One inescapable feature of the later decades of the twentieth century has, for example, been the resurgence of Islam on a global scale, a transformation that has crucial resonance for *both* the relationships between Christian and Muslims in Africa *and* the academic study of these. Undoubtedly a major theme for Africanists in the twenty-first century (as indeed for scholars of religion in Europe), this – regrettably – can be signalled only in passing.

THE AFRICAN DIASPORA

The immediate task is to look in more detail at the African diaspora, with particular attention to its growing presence in Europe. The dispersal of Africans across the globe has been one of the largest and most brutal movements of people that has taken place in modern times – a fact almost entirely explained by the slave trade, which displaced huge numbers of black people to Latin America (notably Brazil), the Caribbean and North

America. The impact on both the sending and receiving societies was incalculable as an economic, social and religious transformation took place. The manner of embedding was, however, very different in the different parts of the New World, contrasts which reflect very immediately the themes developed in the two previous chapters.

The New World

In North America, for example, African forms of religion rapidly became part of the hugely diverse religious market described in Chapter Two. Newly arrived slaves were forbidden to practise their own religion and were introduced instead to Protestantism, with the intention that this would legitimise their enslaved condition, from which they would escape only into eternal life. Such controls were only partially successful: Protestant Christianity offered the hope of freedom in this world too, becoming at the same time an important vehicle for the expression of Africanness (notably in worship). The influence of distinctive forms of black Protestantism on American life was, in consequence, immense. Evangelical rather than liberal in its orientations, it provided none the less crucial motivations for the civil rights movement (not least for Martin Luther King himself). Half a century later African-American Christians remain a major component in the religious life of the United States. For the most part they are to be found in distinctive black-led groups: roughly divided between Baptists (the largest number), Methodists and Pentecostals.

In Latin America (more especially in Brazil) something rather different has happened. Here the influence of traditional African religion can still be seen alongside more orthodox forms of Christianity (an argument in favour of continuity). Significant numbers of Brazilians of African descent belong, for example, to the Afro-Brazilian movements already referred to in Chapter Three, notably Candomblé and Umbanda – movements in

Afro-American Christians: Baptist, Methodists & Pentacostalist

which the question of syncretism (always an ambiguous term) inevitably arises. Syncretism becomes in fact a major theme in Peter Clarke's extensive collection of work in this area (Clarke 1998). Clarke has gathered together a series of empirical studies which highlight the ways in which African and African-derived religions manifest themselves in the contemporary world, underlining for special attention 'their continued dynamism and their relationship with other religions, often labeled syncretism' (1998: viii). There is, following Clarke, no alternative to careful empirical study in order to map, over the long term, the relationship between movements such as Candomblé and Umbanda and the host society (including its religious dimensions). A crucial element in this evolution turns out, once again, to be the growing presence of Pentecostalism in Latin America. As Pentecostals have demanded a discrete space for themselves in Brazilian society, other religious groups have followed suit, a trend noticeable in the religious self-ascriptions (including those to Afro-Brazilian movements) that can be found in the Brazilian census.[14]

Clarke's case studies include Latin America, the Caribbean, the United States and finally Europe – the new field of enquiry. The experience of Africans in the Caribbean provides a stepping stone in this process. In terms, initially, of the new world, the Caribbean case lies somewhere between that of the United States and that of Latin America; outcomes vary depending on whether the dominant religion in the receiving society was Protestant or Catholic. The delicate interaction between host culture and incoming groups becomes in fact the key to understanding the evolution of both Christian and non-Christian groups in this area, where different islands had different policies in terms of conversion. Hence the presence of significant Christian groups in Jamaica and Barbados (with a growing Pentecostal element within them) contrasted with religions that derive more directly from African sources: for example, Santeria, Voodoo and, most important of all, Rastafarianism. The Ethiopian symbolism within the latter picks up once again the crucial significance of

Europe: The Exceptional Case

Ethiopia for African religious movements, outside as well as inside the continent.

Modern Europe

Varieties of Afro-Caribbean religions now have a significant presence in Britain as well as in the West Indies, unsurprisingly given the importance of the Afro-Caribbean population to the British economy in the early post-war decades. This significant migration, from new world to old, becomes moreover the route by which this chapter returns to its starting point: that is to an emphasis on the growing number of Africans in Europe, the particular nature of their religious life, and the disturbing effect that this is beginning to have on the assumed relationship between African and European. In the following paragraphs, particular attention will be paid to the British (moderately long-term) and Dutch (very recent) examples.

Caribbean and African immigrations into Britain are relatively well documented; so too the vibrant church life of these communities in many of Britain's larger cities. There are two sides to this story: first the kind of Christianity that immigrant groups brought with them, but second – and crucially – the initial rejection of the migrant Christians by the established denominations in Britain (for the most part in England). The phenomenal growth of black-led churches was the direct consequence of the latter (Gerloff 1992) – congregations which grew first by immigration, then for demographic reasons, but finally by receiving 'converts' from the historic churches. Such churches become, moreover, an indispensable focus for the cultural identity of their communities, the more so given the very difficult economic and social conditions in which these populations are obliged to live.

Denominationally, however, they are extremely diverse. Gerloff (1992), for example, identifies eleven different traditions, by far the largest being the Pentecostals, themselves divided

Rejection + black-led churches in England
– of great variety

into three families (with sub-groups). The remainder include Methodists, Baptists, Sabbatarians, the Holiness Movements, a significant group of AICs (notably from Nigeria and Ghana) and lastly the British Rastafarian movement. The material needs, finally, to be amplified by data from the mainstream churches in which significant numbers of Africans continue to work despite everything, some in positions of leadership – quite possibly, given the parochial (in the sense of territorial) nature of these churches, in closer contact with the wider population than their counterparts in the black-led churches.

If the experience in Britain (and more especially England) has been longer than most, that in The Netherlands is recent. The study of African immigrant communities in a number of Dutch cities has become, however, the focus of Ter Haar's work on the African diaspora in Europe, with which we started this chapter. The main focus of this account lies in a developed study of the Ghanaian community in the Bijlmer, a suburb of Amsterdam,[15] which becomes de facto an illustration of the wider experience of Africans in Europe. In understanding this process, an initial remark is crucial: that is the centrality of religion to this experience, a characteristic often overlooked by the Western enquirer. In marked contrast to the Africans themselves, for example, 'scholars writing on immigrant communities often define these almost exclusively in terms of ethnicity and ethnic adherence' (Ter Haar 1998b: iii). The primary aim of Ter Haar's work becomes, therefore, the study of recently arrived African immigrant communities in light of their religious affiliations, seeing these not as something exotic or alien but as an increasingly important feature of European society itself.

The Dutch experience (just like the British) needs to be placed in the historical context outlined above: that is the considerable involvement of Dutch entrepreneurs in the trans-Atlantic slave trade, legitimated at times by the selective application of Calvinist theology – activities which exemplify par excellence the role of Europeans as senders. The point to grasp some three hundred

Ghanaians in Amsterdam

years later is the movement of people in a different direction, bringing large numbers from West Africa (and more particularly from Ghana) to many parts of Europe previously unaffected by immigration from the South. For the African, this is part of an ongoing process: West Africans have travelled to find work for generations, but not until now to Europe. It is, moreover, these labour migrants who are largely responsible for the flourishing African Christian congregations in The Netherlands (and indeed elsewhere) at the start of the twenty-first century.

This, however, is only half the story. The other half lies in spiritual rather than economic motivations. For many African Christians, migration to Europe is not simply an economic necessity; it is seen in addition as a God-given opportunity to evangelise – more precisely to reinvigorate the religious lives of those who brought the gospel to Africa in the first place, but who have subsequently gone astray (Ter Haar 1999a: 167). Hence the notion of 'reversed mission', an aspiration eloquently captured in an organisation such as GATE, that is the Gospel from Africa to Europe (an acronym which can also be used theologically to symbolise a pathway to new life).

The paradoxes that follow are considerable, not least the very real difficulties that such churches have in finding accommodation, in a part of Amsterdam built in the 1960s with only one church building to house the mainstream denominations of that area.[16] Burgeoning African congregations, in contrast, cannot find space for their Sunday worship (Ter Haar 1998a: 158). Their churches provide, moreover, a crucial social network for African migrants, offering once again an excellent illustration of the effectiveness of Pentecostal churches (for such they mostly are) in conditions of extreme economic uncertainty. Just as in Africa, they are able to provide the religious beliefs, spiritual resources and social contacts that are necessary not only to survive in a hostile environment, but in some cases to begin the long climb towards respectability within it. If in so doing the tightly-bounded, seemingly undemocratic nature of these

'reversed mission'

Social solidarity, economic survival

churches offends the egalitarian sensibilities of the host population, then so be it.

Ter Haar offers a useful shorthand to draw the threads not only of her own work, but of this chapter together. The 'I' in AICs gradually mutates through the course of time – from 'independent', through 'indigenous', through African 'instituted' or 'initiated' churches to, finally, 'international'. Each shift denotes a different perspective. The current appellation (already seen in the Nigerian case study above) reflects once again the essentially international distribution of Pentecostalism at the start of the twenty-first century, not least in its African forms. Acknowledging that these churches are international just as much as they are African (and so effectively marginalised from the European mainstream) requires, however, from the European a certain reciprocity. It requires, in fact, a willingness to reconstruct the relationships outlined in the introductory pages of this chapter. The implications are immense: 'mission in reverse' – if taken seriously – would turn the traditional relationship between African-European, not to mention the responsibilities that go with it, on its head. It hasn't happened yet.

Documenting the arrival of increasing numbers of Africans into Europe is an incipient field in the study of African religion. It can be found, for instance, in a series of recently held European conferences on the significance of the African Christian diaspora in Europe – in Leeds and Västerås (Sweden) in 1997, Glay (France) and Hamburg in 1998 and in Cambridge in 1999. The papers from the latter have been brought together in a recent volume of the *International Review of Mission*[17] guest edited by Roswith Gerloff. As Gerloff insists, 'South has come North', reversing the demographic trend and bringing new religious ideas into Europe. Such ideas disturb the European mind wedded amongst other things to linear structures and the need to distinguish between the spiritual and the material. African missions, on the other hand:

communal + charismatic

travel along pre-existing social relations such as family, friend-
ship, village or island community, and trade and work
comradeship. They rest on charismatic leadership, communi-
cate in songs and signals, and understand the human person
in his or her relationship to community. Therefore faith
becomes the light, reliable and comforting baggage in the
process of migration and crisis. (Gerloff 2000: 277)

I am well aware that such accounts can be romanticised, just like
those of the AICs in Africa in the mid post-war decades. Despite
this, the presence of African churches in Europe needs to be
taken very seriously. In terms of the religious life of Europe,
these congregations have a very particular position. Almost
uniquely, they exhibit a dual nature: in terms of their Christianity
they are part of the mainstream, but in terms of their vitality,
their distinctive styles of worship and their capacities to discon-
cert, they exemplify the features of an immigrant community
(Davie 2000a: 149). Hence their undoubted significance in the
continuing evolution of Christianity in this part of the world.

Chapter Five

ooooooooooooooooooo

DIASPORA POPULATIONS:
CHRISTIAN COMMUNITIES IN
THE FAR EAST

Up to now the emphasis in this book has been on majority Christian populations, some of which are beginning to display increasing religious pluralism as significant other-faith communities arrive in their midst – European societies are themselves an excellent example. The accommodation of such minorities within an historically Christian culture presents crucially important issues, already touched on in earlier chapters. The fragmentation within Christianity itself has provided a parallel theme. In Latin America, for example, a solidly Catholic culture has begun to dissolve, the catalyst in this instance being rapidly expanding Pentecostalism; in Africa (South of the Sahara) there were several layers of Christian evolution to bear in mind if the present was to be properly understood. Still sticking to the principal theme of systematic comparison with the European case, it is now time to turn to an entirely different religious environment – to a part of the world, that is, where Christians have been a minority rather than a majority, a situation which provokes a very different set of sociological questions.

The three societies in question are, moreover, very different from each other. The Philippines (a developing rather than developed nation) are in many ways similar to Latin America.

They are the only predominantly Christian society in South-east Asia, collectively Christianised (like Latin America) in the sixteenth century at the time of the Spanish circumnavigation of the world. Some four and a half centuries later, the Spanish ceded their claim to the Americans enabling an increased Protestant (as opposed to Catholic) influence – an element which began to grow exponentially in the eighties and nineties, a by now familiar theme though the timing is a little different in each case. An important Muslim minority exists mainly in the south of the Philippines, provoking from time to time a desire for regional political autonomy, a factor which was not present in the Latin American case. The Muslim minority is all the more significant given the much larger, and at times aggressive Muslim presence in South-east Asia.

Korea – or to be more precise South Korea – has experienced an entirely different evolution. Here the dramatic growth in Christianity has been relatively recent (i.e. post-war), though the beginnings of Christian influence go back two centuries or more. The important point to grasp is that the coming of Christianity, notably in its Protestant forms, has accompanied modernisation (not least extremely rapid urbanisation) rather than opposed this, a fact which prompts renewed reflection with regard to the presumed connections between religion (more especially Christianity) and modernity. Are these necessarily incompatible? In Korea it appears otherwise, though a series of political factors should also be taken into account. In Korea, certain forms of Christianity have undoubtedly formed a bulwark first against Japanese imperialism and later against the communist North. Religion and politics become increasingly entangled in a nation which represented (and in some respects still does represent) the front line in the confrontation of the West with communism.

A final, very much briefer illustration comes from Melanesia.

It offers a particularly colourful example of reversed roles, thus reinforcing the argument of the African case study. It forms a bridge to a re-consideration of the European case in the more theoretical concluding chapter.

THE PHILIPPINES — VARIATIONS ON THE LATIN THEME

It has been considerably harder to find up-to-date information about the religious situation in the Philippines than about the other case studies covered in this book, though quite why this should be so is more difficult to say. The statistical framework is none the less available (Barrett *et al.* 2001) and offers a useful starting point before turning to more qualitative material. About 85 per cent of the Philippino population are members of the Catholic Church — the largest proportion of Catholics of any country in Asia. This has been the case since the conversion of the Philippines en masse by the Spanish in the sixteenth century. Equally (perhaps more) significant, however, is the nature of the Catholicism found there: its dramatic and demonstrative character, especially noticeable in Holy Week and often embodying folk as well as Christian beliefs, has become the focus of journalistic as well as scholarly accounts. Some examples will be given below.

Before doing so, a second numerical indicator of the continuing pervasiveness of Catholicism, and especially among young people, can be found in the comparative statistics available for the biennial meeting of the Catholic World Youth Days. These meetings, at which the Pope himself is present, are intended for young Catholics worldwide; they are held every two years (more or less), each time in a different venue. The following figures (normally taken at the final mass) are instructive in themselves:[1]

1987	Buenos Aires, Brazil	900,000
1989	Santiago de Compostella, Spain	400,000
1991	Czestochowa, Poland	1,600,000
1993	Denver, United States	600,000
1995	Manila, The Philippines	4,000,000
1997	Paris, France	1,000,000
2000	Rome, Italy	2,000,000

Even more convincing, however, are the eye-witness accounts of the Philippino meeting. The following statement, for example, gives some idea of what it was like to be in a crowd of four million people:

> I was an invited guest to the final mass of the World Youth Day in the Philippines in 1995, in my capacity as General Secretary of the NCC (National Council of Churches) Philippines. The crowd was so thick, the thickest that I have ever seen or experienced, including sporting events, that I could not walk through the crowd to reach the stage. The Pope could not be driven to the stage, he was helicoptered in. I do not think I will ever see as large a crowd as that one. Four million is a fair estimate. Where in the world can you ever see a crowd as large, and this was five o'clock in the morning! This phenomenon simply convinced me of the incredible drawing power that the Church has, and continues to have in the country – something that no other institution has. (Cariño 2001, private communication)

The drawing power of the Catholic Church becomes in fact a repeating theme throughout this section; it is an important key to understanding the religious situation in the Philippines.

In addition to the official Catholic Church, however, there are a variety of indigenous movements. Two of these – the Iglesia Filipina Independiente (IFI) and the Iglesia ni Kristo (InK) – are particularly influential. The former flourished at the turn of the twentieth century when anti-colonialism was at its height.

Thereafter the numbers stagnated as the tide of nationalism receded and, more specifically, after 1906 when the Supreme Court ordered the return of all Catholic properties appropriated by the Independent Church. In the late 1930s, however, a new Declaration of Faith and Articles of Religion were prepared, which resulted in closer links between the IFI and the (Anglican) Philippine Episcopal Church, not least the mutual recognition of their 'holy orders' – a highly significant move which enabled the IFI to use Episcopal seminaries for the training of their clergy. The two churches, though still fully independent, entered into communion with one another in 1961. After a long period of relative decline (given the increase in the population as a whole), the Independent Church is once again experiencing growth – its membership in 2000 was between four and five million.

The second of these churches – the Iglesia ni Kristo – is very different. It was established in 1914 by a former Catholic who felt called to revive the original Christian Church, outside of which there is no salvation; it is an aggressively nationalistic movement with an all-Philippino leadership but with congregations overseas as well as at home. Currently this highly visible (architecturally amongst other things) Church has 8,400 congregations made up mainly of poor people. Freston (2000: 71) characterises it as 'neither Catholic nor Protestant but "evangelical" '; he notes in addition the recent influence of the Iglesia ni Kristo in Philippino politics (partly through the mechanism of bloc voting).

Mainstream Protestant missionaries from outside and from a wide variety of denominations began to arrive around 1900, encouraged by American colonial rule. Both the number of the missionaries and the denominational mix have grown rapidly since the Second World War resulting in a marked expansion of Protestantism in the same period. This expansion became an explosion in the 1980s and 1990s as Pentecostal and charismatic movements spread rapidly both inside and outside the established

~ Pentacostalism

Table 5.1 Number of non-Catholic religious groups registered in the Philippines

	Metro Manila	Outside Metro Manila	Nationwide
Before 1980	111	117	228
After 1980	836	612	1448
Total	947	729	1676

The numbers of actual Protestant church congregations were 1970: 5000, 1980: 9400, and 1990: 23000.
Figures taken from *Dawn Research Report* 1991.

churches. This is, undoubtedly, the fastest growing sector of the Philippino religious economy as it is in Latin America, though much less has been written about it. One sympathetic commentator (Miranda-Feliciano 1991) speaks, however, of exponential church growth, a movement that embraces both evangelical Protestants and charismatic Catholics. Impressive statistics support this statement both at a micro and macro level (see Table 5.1).

So far then, the story is similar to that described in Chapter Three, in terms both of the Catholic culture of the society as a whole and the phenomenal growth of new churches (notably Pentecostalism) in recent decades.

Rather different is the significant Muslim presence in the Philippines (about 5 per cent of the total population), a constituency which is concentrated in the southern islands, forming in some places a majority in the local population. It is important to remember that a Muslim presence in the area predates the arrival of Christianity by more than a century, though it is not indigenous. From the mid-fourteenth century, Islam had been spreading northwards from Indonesia (largely as the result of trading links) and was well established in the south of the Philippines by the time that the Spaniards arrived. Despite attempts at Christianisation (similar to those in Spain herself), the Muslims maintained themselves on the island of Mindaneo and in the Sulu archipelago,[2] a resistance which continued under the American occupation. Since independence the situation has remained tense leading to armed revolt on Mindaneo in the 1970s. Policies of Christian settlement leading to declining control by Philippino Muslims have been balanced by increasing support from neighbouring (and not so close) Muslim countries, a process which has both strengthened Muslim consciousness in the area and encouraged the idea of regional autonomy for the southern islands. In the late 1980s, following the restoration of democracy, the Moro National Liberation Front entered into negotiations with the Aquino and Ramos governments; the smaller Muslim movements have, however, been more resistant to compromise, still anxious to maintain the ideal of an independent Muslim state.

So much for the statistical outline, which can now be fleshed out by more qualitative accounts. With respect to Catholicism, these are written from different points of view. One source can be found in the work of missiologists whose primary concern lies in understanding the Philippino mentality with a view to sympathetic evangelism. Maggay (1998) offers an interesting example. She describes what Philippinos call 'fold Christianity', 'a product of pre-Hispanic religious imagination and Catholicism of the Iberian variety, a branch of Christianity untouched by the upheavals of the Reformation and unscrutinized by the radical doubt of the Age of Reason' (1998: 362). One result of this lies in the huge cultural gap between the Philippino consciousness and the more cerebral, word-centred forms of Protestantism brought by some missionaries. In contrast charismatic movements (both Catholic and Protestant) find it considerable easier to engage with local people for whom a religion of power has particular resonance.

A more detailed and primarily anthropological account of

Philippino Catholicism can be found in a special issue on the Philippines of the *Review of Indonesian and Malaysian Affairs*. The focus of this article is a well-known but hitherto poorly studied religious practice – the Morion festival which takes place on the island of Marinduque during Holy Week (Adachi 1994).[3] The festival is one of many religious dramas enacted at this time, a period in the year permeated by the atmosphere of the passion and resurrection of Christ when the preoccupations of everyday life are put on one side. It differs, however, from other examples in that the festival is not (or not fully) sanctioned by the Catholic Church. For the islanders, on the other hand, the Church's official position is relatively unimportant. Despite (or maybe because of) their participation in the Morion festival, they consider themselves fully Christian. It is this amalgam of Christian and folk elements which fascinates Adachi.

The Morion festival is based on a biblical story, the piercing of Christ's side by a Roman solder (John 19:19–34). The associated legend maintains that a drop of blood from the crucified Christ spurted into the eyes of Longinius, a Roman soldier, miraculously curing him from blindness and thereby converting him to Christianity. Adachi describes the events of Holy Week which commemorate this episode in some detail. From Holy Monday, Morions roam the town dressed (and masked) as Roman centurions. They are obliged to keep moving despite the intensity of the summer heat – a way of giving thanks to God for their survival through illness or misfortune. On Holy Wednesday and Good Friday, Morions participate in two processions organised by the Catholic Church, the route of which symbolically connects the different districts of the town. Central to Good Friday, moreover, is the practice of the *antipo*, a demanding form of self-flagellation (now frowned upon by the hierarchy), into which Morions and other penitents are drawn, symbolising a further giving of thanks or atonement for past sins.[4] The week's events come to a climax on Easter morning when the capture and martyrdom of Longinius are ebulliently re-enacted. Before he dies, Longinius refuses to deny his faith and recounts how the blood of the Saviour restored sight to his blind eye; his body, finally, is borne in a funeral procession around the town – the cycle of death and resurrection is once more complete.

The long-term evolution of this festival is interesting in itself. It dates from the 1870s and initially represented an attempt by the Catholic Church (more especially the Augustinian Recollects) to encourage participation in Catholic ritual. The more penitential aspects came later, during the American occupation. Adachi argues (1994: 26) that this shift was only partly a corrective introduced by the Church; it also incorporated peasant conceptions of suffering, some of which drew from traditional spirit cults rather than, or in addition to, Christianity. Whatever the reasons, the event grew in popularity during this period and established the format of the current festival. The evolution of the festival since independence (it was suppressed during the Japanese occupation) is equally revealing. Two rather different things happened at once: firstly the Church attempted to distance itself, particularly from the excesses of the penitential practices (one result of this has been the moving of the festival away from the square beside the church); and secondly – especially in the sixties and seventies – the festival received a considerable boost as a tourist attraction in a part of the Philippines where tourism represents an important sector of the economy. The reaction of the Church to the latter phenomenon has been mixed: on the one hand it is understandably critical of increasing commercialisation but at the same time cannot ignore the growing prominence of the festival in local affairs. The emphasis is now on transformation rather than proscription.

Obviously different interest groups approach this event with different motives; it remains a site of contention. One thing is clear, however, there is absolutely no evidence here of secularisation. Philippinos are and remain a deeply religious population. Forms of religion may mutate over time and acquire different meanings, but they do not disappear. An equally persuasive

evolution, but no
secularisation

Communal Christianity (handwritten)
of small groups is booming (handwritten)

body of evidence resistant to the notion of secularisation can,
moreover, be seen in the emergence of Pentecostalism, indeed
of the charismatic movement in general, in the last decades of
the twentieth century.

Miranda-Feliciano's article is useful in this respect; its descrip-
tions and examples cross the denominational divide, but 'we are
not speaking here of traditional Christian religiosity or rituals'
(1991: 64). The emphasis rather is on small Bible-based groups
(with and without pastors), in which healing and exorcism play
a central part, and where prayers are answered, miracles expected
and deliverance experienced. It is these phenomena that lie at
the heart of the unprecedented church growth evident in the
Philippines from the 1980s onwards and which, it seems, appeal
to the Philippino population rather more readily than pro-
positional Protestantism. There is also (as in both Latin America
and Africa) the attractiveness of the tightly-bound and supportive
group in precarious economic conditions, including extremely
rapid urbanisation.

Of course there are questions as well as answers in the ensuing
discussions (as there were in the Latin American chapter), not
least from those who have had a longstanding commitment to
the renewal of society and social structures (Philippino forms of
liberation theology), and from those who have particular reason
to be suspicious of American influence (in a part of the world
where the United States has played a major role). There is also,
following both Miranda-Feliciano (1991) and Maggay (1998),
criticism of (a) 'health and wealth' preaching and (b) too great
an emphasis on feelings. And with particular reference to the
latter perceptive Philippino commentators wonder about the
superficial nature of many conversions. What, they ask, will
happen to the rapidly multiplying new churches in the longer
term? (Interestingly, exactly the same question will arise in the
section relating to Korea.) So far, however, the indicators in
the Philippines continue to rise.

The relationship between the political sphere and different

the dangers (handwritten)

forms of religious life in the Philippines is particularly controversial, just as it is in Latin America; there can be no doubt
about that. The crucial point to grasp, however – over and above
the frequently disputed detail (Freston 2001: 74–5) – is the
continuing significance of the religious factor in the *public* as
well as private lives of Philippinos, despite the fact that Church
and State are officially separate and have been since the coming
of American rule at the end of the nineteenth century.[5] The
separation of Church and State is one thing; the ongoing political
life of the country quite another, a point strongly confirmed by
Cariño in a personal communication. For the purposes of this
chapter, the latter point can be clearly illustrated with reference
to two defining moments in the evolution of Philippino politics
in the final decades of the twentieth century: those that have
become known as EDSA Uno and EDSA Dos.[6] Churches and
church-people were heavily involved in both.

EDSA Uno occurred in 1986, bringing onto the streets all
those many and varied sections of the population who opposed
the dictatorship of President Marcos. The Catholics, spearheaded
by Cardinal Sin, were a crucial element in this process – more
specifically, the Cardinal called on the faithful to join with 'our
friends' (including significant representation of the police and
the military) to put an end to a 'reign of evil' (Cariño 2000: 2).
They were supported in this enterprise by most mainstream
Protestants, grouped around the National Council of Churches
of the Philippines. The growing numbers of evangelicals were,
however, more divided and whatever the distaste they felt for
Marcos himself, the assertion that the victory of the people
against Marcos was a Marian event was seen as provocative in
groups for whom anti-Catholicism is a significant element (Rose
1996: 323). The latter sentiments are undoubtedly important.
Even more crucial, however, is the need to realise that without
the pulling power of the Catholic Church, such gatherings could
not, very probably, have taken place at all (and certainly not on

the scale that they did). Their scale, moreover, was a principal reason for their effectiveness.

EDSA Dos is much more recent (2001), focusing this time on the need to remove President Estrada from office.[7] Once again the groups that took part represented many aspects of Philippino life including the churches. But this time the divisions were rather more marked, in so far as significant numbers of evangelicals (though by no means all) and indeed some Catholics saw in Estrada the protector of the poor and were ready to offer support rather than opposition to the beleaguered president. Indeed following Rose (1996: 339), it is probably more accurate to see the lines of political demarcation at the turn of the century increasingly running through the denominations rather than between them. You cannot, in other words, simply read off political allegiance from confessional attachment. Religio-political connections are considerably more complex than that, in a field which requires ongoing and careful scrutiny given its undisputed importance to Philippino life.

Cariño (2000) makes a further perceptive comment regarding the modalities of political movements. Between EDSA Uno and EDSA Dos, the technology of protest shifted from the radio to the mobile phone. In this respect Philippino political organising both reflects and makes use of developed global technology. Different religious groups are as much part of this evolution as anyone else, offering yet another illustration of the evident compatibility, in the Philippino context, between the modernising process (albeit a very uneven one) and the continued significance of religion at every level of society. With this in mind, it seems that the discourse of secularisation must, once again, be put firmly on one side.

South Korea constitutes an entirely different and better documented case (and infinitely more so for those able to use Korean sources). It is, and always has been, a multi-religious nation as layer upon layer of religious life form and reform over millennia rather than centuries. The oldest religious traditions can be found in ancestor worship and shamanism, elements of which became incorporated in both Buddhism (dominant in Korea from the fourth to the fourteenth centuries) and in Confucianism which supplanted Buddhism as the national religion in the fourteenth century and continued as such until the Japanese occupation in 1910. Christianity entered the field relatively late – Catholic congregations date back to the late eighteenth century, Protestant missionaries arrived some hundred years later. The early beginnings of Protestant Christianity still resonate, in, for example, the influence of missionary establishments on the education system. The really dramatic growth of Protestantism (and up to a point of Catholicism) comes, however, at the end of the twentieth century. It is not an exaggeration to say that the religious landscape of South Korea has been transformed as a result.[8]

The bare bones of this transformation, the focus of this section, are indicated in Table 5.2.[9] A word of caution is necessary, however, before jumping to conclusions about these figures. Statistics for Christian and non-Christian religious groups in Korea are not directly comparable in that terms such as membership are understood differently in the different faith groups. Information that believers provide about themselves, for example, differs markedly from the numbers reported by the religious communities (Yoon 1997, Daiber 2000). This mismatch is not quite the same as that encountered in the American case, where respondents (unlike their European counterparts) were

Christianty Transfms religious
landscape of S. Korea in late 20th century

Table 5.2 Religious change in South Korea 1962–94

	Protestantism growth rate (%)		Catholicism growth rate (%)		Buddhism growth rate (%)	
1962	736,000		590,000		687,000	
1970	3,192,000	333.7	779,000	32.0	4,943,000	619.5
1985	6,489,000	103.3	1,865,000	139.4	8,059,000	63.0
1991	8,037,000	23.9	2,476,000	32.8	11,729,000	45.5
1994	8,146,000	1.4	2,640,000	6.6	10,921,000	− 6.9

Table reproduced from Kim (2002). Original figures taken from *The Yearbook of Korean Religion* (1993) for the years 1962 and 1970, and from *Social Indicators in Korea* (1999) for the years 1985, 1991 and 1994.

anxious to give the impression that they are regular churchgoers even if they are not. In Korea, it is the categories themselves that are inappropriate in a population that thinks very differently about religion. Following Daiber, the system works relatively well for Buddhism and Christianity, but very much less so for Confucianism. The significance of shamanism disappears altogether in a statistical table, in that it is not considered a 'religion' as such; conversely the number of Koreans who appear to have no religion at all is exaggerated.

These are important issues and should be kept in mind through the following discussion. The recent and dramatic growth in the Christian sector of Korean society cannot, however, be denied. It requires close scrutiny – once again at the level of data (the facts that are available to us) and explanation (why did this very dramatic change take place?). The growth, for a start, is uneven. The real take-off in the Protestant churches[10] occurs in the 1960s and 1970s; thereafter it slows to the point of stagnation in the 1990s. The growth in Catholicism, in contrast, starts later but continues longer, albeit at a slower rate than in earlier decades.

Buddhism grows in parallel,
— all along with economic growth

It is important, finally, not to forget the parallel growth in
Buddhism over the same period; this is equally dramatic (indeed
more so) in the 1960s but tails off to the point of decline as the
century comes to a close.[11] All these figures, moreover, need to
be seen against the background of equally impressive economic
growth. South Korea is an Asian tiger par excellence, notwithstanding the recent difficulties in the economic development of
the region.

We are, therefore, confronted with a situation in which rapid
growth in major sections of the religious sphere accompanies
rapid modernisation. Exactly how the two variables are related to
each other is, however, a much more difficult question. Add
to this the specificities of the political situation in this part of the
world and the complexity of the issues begins to become apparent.

In order to understand these better, Kim (2002) takes the
period (1960–2000) more or less a decade at a time and within
this looks first at the Catholic case and then at the different
strands within Protestantism. There are two ways into the argument. The first concerns the background variables that are
common to all faith communities. Extremely rapid economic
growth is the first and most obvious of these; from the 1960s
on, South Korea climbs higher and higher in the international
economic tables (whether of GNP or GNI and in terms of both
gross and per capita indices). In addition, there are significant
political changes over the period as Korea moves from a military
regime in the 1960s and 1970s to a gradual but decisive democratisation in the 1980s. The second part of Kim's article
concentrates on the responses of the different Christian denominations (together with the different theological tendencies within
these) to this shifting economic and political context; responses
that are associated with – or possibly are the reason for – differ-
ential success rates.

The situational factors, both economic and political, can be
taken first. It is true that the economic indicators soared in the

religious growth with
modernisation

— or urbanization + conflict

post-war period (nobody denies this); but so too did the social costs – in terms, first of all, of an extremely rapid movement of people from the country to the cities. The result was an increasing imbalance between rural and urban populations. Mega-cities mushroomed containing populations cut loose from the traditional values of the rural community. (In this respect, the Korean situation is no different from the many others that we have already described.) Related to this was a more generalised conflict between traditional and emergent values, with a strong emphasis on what Kim calls a 'me-ism' or 'we-ism', rather than a developed understanding of individualism with a sense of obligation as well as of rights. Such tensions were exacerbated by the dramatic but uneven rise in per capita income, leading, despite an overall increase in affluence, to growing economic inequalities. All this, moreover, took place in a situation of considerable political uncertainty, dominated by an authoritarian regime which by its very nature inhibited the growth of civil society.

From the 1980s on, however, the atmosphere begins to change as South Korea became increasingly exposed to cultural as well as economic influences from outside, a situation which encouraged not only greater democratisation in the political process, but 'a range of what might be called post-modern characteristics' (Kim 2002). These include greater class differentiation, an increasing complexity of identities, a growing generation gap, and the gradual emergence of civil society. Such changes are accompanied, finally, by a greater emphasis on consumption, a degree of pleasure-seeking, and an invasion of mass culture. A process, moreover, which appears to coincide with a rapid slow-down in church growth, to the point, finally, of stagnation. Why?

Some sort of answer will emerge as we look at the responses of the different Christian communities to the changes in Korean society over the past four decades. The Catholic case is instructive in so far as the post-conciliar Catholic Church in Korea

then slow-slow

emphasised far more than the Protestant denominations both an awareness of and a readiness to value indigenous Korean culture. In the sixties and early seventies, however, such attributes alienated rather than attracted the Korean people intent on maximising Western gains. Catholic growth rates in the mid post-war decades were, in consequence, markedly lower than those in the 1950s. Bit by bit, however, the cultural mood shifted to a greater appreciation of what Catholicism had to offer: not only an endorsement of traditional culture but a greater emphasis on welfare and social justice. Hence an increased growth rate, beginning in the late 1970s but increasing rapidly in the 1980s, a decade in which the Korean Catholic Church doubled in size. As part of the same process, significant numbers of Catholics became involved in the democratisation movement. Cardinal Soo-Hwan Kim, for example, repeatedly underlined the importance of democratisation – as a result MyungDong Cathedral became a centre of political activity (Kang 2000). Catholics, for example, were among those who opposed the government's 4.13 Constitution protection plan, put together in order to consolidate the military regime.[12]

Baker (1997) complements this account with a longer-term and more detailed history of the Catholic Church in Korea. Notable in this evolution is the gradual Koreanisation of the Church, a process that finally comes to fruition in the 1960s, just as the policies of the Second Vatican Council were beginning to make an impact. At the same time (indeed as part of the same process), there is an increasing willingness to intervene in secular affairs, first in terms of the regime itself (thought in the sixties to be dangerously Protestant), but later – in the 1970s and 1980s – involving a direct confrontation with poverty alongside a commitment to human rights, social justice and indeed to democracy itself. Such views were encouraged by a shift in the Catholic population. Partly because of its political stance, Catholicism becomes increasingly attractive to urban intellectuals, helping the Church to shed its rural and backward image –

Europe: The Exceptional Case

Conservative protestantism grew with economy

a shift, in fact, that mirrors the changes taking place in Korean society itself. With this in mind, Baker concludes:

> There have been some remarkable changes in Korea over the last four decades. A poverty-stricken nation has become a force to be reckoned with in world markets. A succession of governments that executes political dissidents has been succeeded by one led by a former prodemocracy activist. And a Roman Catholic Church that once survived on the periphery of society has joined the mainstream. (Baker 1997: 164)

This is no mean achievement, though frequently eclipsed by the explosion in Protestantism over the same period.

Following Kim, Protestants – and more especially conservative Protestants (see note 10) – were the great gainers in the 1960s, effecting their policies at least in part by means of mass evangelistic rallies, themselves underpinned by a theology of church growth which, quite clearly, caught the mood of the moment. Such rallies emphasised individual rather than social salvation and legitimised, indeed encouraged, material blessing; in so doing, they came to represent a form of religion entirely compatible with Western-style modernisation. The combination was powerful; in the 1960s and 1970s conservative Protestant churches grew nearly as fast as the economy itself (see Table 5.2). Among them were the mega-churches of the mega-cities, epitomised by the Yoido Full Gospel Church, reputedly the largest congregation in the world (see below). Part of the attraction undoubtedly lay in the attitude of these churches towards the military regime; refraining from criticism, they implicitly endorsed the status quo, appealing to a population that was more concerned (unsurprisingly at the height of the Cold War) with protection from the communist North than with democratisation as such. Policies which endorsed supposedly left-wing ideas of social justice (espoused amongst others by liberal Protestants[13]) were even less popular.

The balance began to shift in the 1980s, precisely the decade

---

grew with military regime

that had seen the advance of Catholicism in Korean society. Korean people continued to be wary of the liberal option but became increasingly dissatisfied with the almost total lack of social awareness in conservative Protestant theology. It was at this point, moreover, that a greater appreciation of traditional Korean values gradually re-emerged; Western materialism no longer had all the answers – more than this, it was increasingly perceived as the creator just as much as the solver of society's problems. Nor, moreover, was it possible any longer to resist the democratisation process, a movement that had gained an unstoppable momentum in Korean society by the mid 1980s. A theology, finally, that was based on a combination of the pre-modern (authoritarianism and vertical human relationships) and the modern (rigidity and uniformity) looked increasingly out of place in the much more flexible climate that was emerging as the century came to an end.

Bearing such factors in mind, it becomes easier to understand why the amazingly successful package put together by the conservative Protestants no longer attracted the numbers that it did in previous decades. The problem, moreover, was exacerbated by an increasing tendency to schism. Not only were conservative Protestants opposed to liberals, they increasingly succumbed to division amongst themselves. The Catholic Church on the other hand gained in credibility, relatively speaking. By the end of the decade, however, the Christian presence (whether Catholic or Protestant), though undeniably a permanent feature of Korean society – and on a scale unimaginable in the immediate post-war period – is no longer growing. Nor, it is important to remember, is Buddhism, despite an equivalent (perhaps even more dramatic) increase over the same period. Bearing the collective downturn in mind, the situation should, perhaps, engender caution in face of the wilder claims about religious growth at the turn of the millennium whether in Latin America, Africa or the Pacific Rim. It is indeed impressive, but may not continue ad infinitum. Only time will tell.

Others have reflected on the shifts in fortune of conservative Protestantism from the inside. One such comes from an assistant pastor of the Yoido Full Gospel Church (Hong 2000). Reviewing the possibility of stagnation and decline after decades of growth, the author underlines two internal reasons for the slump in the statistics (in addition that is to the shifts in Korean society itself). The first of these concerns an increasing lack of social credibility – largely associated, according to Hong, with corruption and scandals in private and public life. The second lies in the phenomenon of nominalism. Those leaving the conservative Protestant churches often cease to practise any religion at all, indicating a somewhat superficial attachment to the faith in the first place. Both factors, following Hong, are indicative of too great an emphasis on quantity rather than quality in church growth, a stress which leads in turn to the uncritical adoption of particular strategies (size became the only criterion of success) – in many ways a direct reflection of the economic life of Korea over the same period.

The Yoido Full Gospel Church remains none the less a hugely impressive undertaking, so much so that it merits a place in the *Guinness Book of Records* as the fastest-growing church in the world. From humble beginnings as a tent church in 1958, it has grown systematically to 700,000 plus in the 1990s. The exponential growth dates from the 1970s. Luca (2000) offers more detail on the creation and management of this immense Pentecostal congregation (if such is the right word for a community of this size). The story is remarkable, first of all, in geographical and architectural terms. In the 1970s (after repeated relocations) the Full Gospel Church became the first congregation to build on the Island of Yoido (also the home of the national parliament); architecturally similar, the two buildings face each other, a reward perhaps for repeatedly endorsing nationalistic policies. State-of-the-art technology permits the smooth running of service after service as tens of thousands are ushered in and out of the building on a Sunday morning. Other

Yoido Full Gospel church
now against Parlt. buildg

developments have grown alongside the church – for example, and very selectively, educational facilities (including a television studio); welfare initiatives (for the unemployed and the elderly); a centre for international mission (itself incorporating 'Church Growth International'); and a whole series of local missions (organised by different sectors – defined by profession, social-economic category or cultural interests). The latter represent impressive networks, counteracting many of the negative effects of rapid modernisation. At the same time they are evidence of an emergent second generation, markedly more prosperous than the disadvantaged groups initially attracted to the church.[14]

Something of the initial character of the venture (the tent church) is, however, maintained in the 'Prayer Mountain' some thirty kilometres from Seoul, where individuals or groups can retreat for a period of intensive prayer in rather simpler conditions. Even this, however, can accommodate 10,000 people in either Korean or Western facilities (many visitors come from overseas). Unsurprisingly the Prayer Mountain in itself requires considerable levels of practical as well as spiritual organisation, not least the shuttle buses that run to and fro from the city centre.

One 'frequently asked question' concerns the explosion of Christian activity in South Korea, compared with the relative inactivity in this respect of Korea's Asian neighbours – especially Japan.[15] Are there, in other words, particular features of Korean society which explain the predilection of the Korean population for new and, in the case of Christianity, Western forms of religion in the twentieth century? The answer lies at least in part in the political evolution of the region. In the early twentieth century, Christianity grew in popularity under the Japanese occupation of Korea. Traditional Confucian values had failed to withstand the foreign invasion, itself a great humiliation, in the face of which Protestant values were seen as a means of transformation. Yong-Shin Park (2000) documents this episode in some detail, also explaining the profound effects, both direct

Christianity and S. Korean nationalism in the 20th c.

and indirect, that Protestants and Protestant missions had on the society of which it had become part. It was in this context that the contribution to the educational system had such a decisive impact. Protestantism found itself, moreover, in the happy position of representing modernity but not representing a colonialist threat (Freston 2001: 63) – quite clearly the threat lay elsewhere, in the aggression of the Japanese. This combination of factors, Freston argues, is unique in this part of the world, unlikely to be repeated elsewhere.

Something like it was, however, repeated in the post-war period, and more particularly after the Korean war. As Korea divided between the South (supported by the West, notably the United States) and the North (supported by the communist world), the Protestant churches became a crucial factor in the emergent polarisation – for good or ill. There was, first of all, a considerable relocation of Christians to the South; there was in addition material support from the Americans, encouraging amongst other things the proliferation of denominations and a tendency to schism; there was, finally, a marked effect on the political life of the country as a whole and the role of Protestants within this. The military regime was endorsed by many, though by no means all Protestants, as the bulwark against communism, despite its own anti-democratic tendencies.[16]

In some respects, therefore, though considerable caution is needed in such comparisons, Christianity – and more particularly Protestantism – comes to play a role in South Korea which is rather similar to that of the Catholic Church in Ireland and in Poland (see Chapter One). In all three case, there is 'extra' work for the churches to do, quite apart from their role as the carrier of a particular theology; they come to represent the identity of the nation in face of external opposition. Two questions follow from this. One has already been mentioned: that is the uniqueness of the Korean case amongst the societies of the Pacific Rim and, in consequence, the need to be careful about generalising from this. The second concerns the future: what will happen next, as the threat from the North recedes? Both Park (2000) and Freston (2001) raise this point at the end of their respective accounts of Korean Protestantism. Already experiencing setbacks after a quite extraordinary period of numerical growth, will these churches and their leaders find within themselves the resources to face an entirely different future?

One further point should be mentioned in conclusion – the presence of Korean missionaries all over the world. An emphasis on overseas mission is, in fact, nothing new in Korean Protestantism; it dates from the late nineteenth century. The practice fell into abeyance, however, between 1900 and 1970 (unsurprisingly given the poverty of the Korean Church), only to re-emerge with the shift in fortunes of Protestantism in Korea itself. From this point on, the number of missionaries increases fast, from 94 in 1969, to 3272 in 1994, to an estimated 6800 in 2000 (Park 1997: 330, using figures from official church handbooks). Destinations (in descending order of numbers) include Asia, Eurasia (including Russia), Latin America, Europe, the Pacific, the Middle East, the Caribbean and North America. Some missionaries work with Korean congregations living abroad (in the US, for example, where the number of Koreans is very large), but others with indigenous people.

A rather more analytical account of the same phenomenon can be found in Clark (1997) who documents the various waves of Korean missionary activity in recent decades, noting in particular (a) the phenomenal growth in the 1980s, brought about very largely by the lifting of restrictions relating to currency exchange (sending bodies could now keep missionaries in the field for longer periods) and (b) the particular contribution of the Yoido Full Gospel Church to the missionary endeavour as a whole. Clark also stresses an alternative strategy which dates back to the 1970s, i.e. in the creation of training organisations in Korea to which aspiring Christians from the third world were invited. Either way, internationalisation and globalisation (essential features of modernity) are readily embraced by the

Young Melanesian Brothers in Exeter

Korean churches leading once again to the inescapable conclusion. In South Korea, just as in the Philippines, there is no incompatibility between the modernising process and vibrant ‖‖ forms of religious life. The reverse is, if anything, the case.

MELANESIAN MISSIONARIES

The final example in this chapter is very much briefer but develops the concluding theme of the previous section. It derives from the connections between Exeter (a monocultural, somewhat traditional English city) and the Anglican Church in Melanesia. In the summer of 2000, this city received a visit from a contingent of Melanesian Anglicans, to be more precise a group of *young men* from the Melanesian Brotherhood – a demographic category notably absent from the active participants in the Church of England. The Melanesian Brotherhood was founded in 1925; its main purpose was evangelistic (taking the gospel to the remote islands and villages of the Solomon Islands). In order to achieve this goal, its members lived (and continue to live) as 'brothers' to the people, respecting their traditions and customs and helping with everyday activities – such as fishing, harvesting and house-building. The Brothers take vows of poverty, chastity and obedience for a period of five years, after which the vows can be renewed.[17] The group came to Exeter at the invitation of the Bishop, but in part to pay homage to Bishop Patterson, one of the founders of Anglicanism in Melanesia, who served his title in Alfington, a small village in the Diocese of Exeter. Bishop Patterson was eventually martyred on the island of Nakapu (in 1871), a moment captured in a frieze on the nave pulpit in Exeter Cathedral.

Anglicans in the Diocese of Melanesia, it should be remembered, remain active rather than nominal members of their Church, quite unlike the current state of their *fons et origo* (a Northern European establishment where relatively small numbers maintain the structures on behalf of the nominal believers). In the South Pacific, in contrast, Christianity (including Anglicanism) retains the kind of vibrancy already described in this and previous chapters, though in forms particular to the region.

In the course of their visit to Exeter, the Melanesian team took part in the scheduled Sunday morning worship in the cathedral, a liturgy which included a dramatic presentation of the gospel. 'Fifteen of the Melanesian Brothers, in traditional South Pacific dress, performed liturgical dances, and provided music on pan pipes and other instruments, probably never heard before in the Cathedral, as part of the Eucharist' (*Cathedral News*, September 2000). Still dressed for this part of the service, their leader then preached from the cathedral pulpit – looking essentially like the 'savage' characteristic of a children's book of the immediate post-war period and right above the frieze which depicted the martyrdom of the Bishop at the hands of a native. At the end of the service the Melanesians 'danced' the congregation and its dignitaries out of the cathedral. This, if ever there was one, was a reversal of roles, a visual example, perhaps, of future possibilities. It is interesting to note that the whole episode was well received by a normally conservative cathedral congregation and reported favourably in the local press. The relationship, moreover, is ongoing: two Melanesian Brothers will spend the year 2001–2 year in the Diocese of Exeter, contributing to the life of the local churches.

The theoretical implications of these shifting roles, as Koreans send missionaries to Asia and beyond and as Anglican Melanesian brothers preach the gospel in English cathedrals, will provide a prominent theme in a final, more analytical chapter.

CONCEPTUAL MAPS

The chapters of this book have been arranged geographically. Each of them has focused on a different part of the world, with the aim of extracting from the discussion the specific ways in which both the Christian churches and the Christian populations of that global region behave, concentrating on the differences between Latin Americans, say, and Europeans. It is now time to gather up some of these themes with the intention of (a) establishing the case for European exceptionalism, (b) asking *why* the patterns of religious behaviour in this part of the world are distinct and (c) whether and in what direction they are likely to change. This is the goal of the first part of the chapter; its structure reflects the different sociological tasks that have already emerged in the more substantive material (most notably in Chapter Two).

A second and crucially important point follows from this. If we are to argue that patterns of religion in Europe are indeed an exceptional case, it is important to ask what they are exceptional to? Is there a norm elsewhere? And if so where and in what does this norm consist? The same point can be put in a different way: Europe may indeed be exceptional in terms of its comparative secularity, but the rest of the world (or more modestly other parts of the Christian world) demonstrate not one but many examples of religious vitality, which are – and this is the crucial point – as different from each other as each of them is from West Europe. It is this question that will be tackled in the second part of the chapter.

The argument at this stage will be rather more abstract in so far as it concentrates on the sociological tools that are necessary to understand the emergent patterns of religion across the world. If it is not possible simply to take the theoretical frames that have developed in Europe or the United States and apply these to all cases, what resources are available to the sociologist in order to understand what is happening? Crucial questions – theoretical and methodological – begin to formulate. An attempt will be made both to articulate these questions more sharply and to set out, at least tentatively, some of the possible answers. The notion of 'conceptual maps' has been deliberately chosen to describe this task, given its geographical as well as sociological resonance.

THE CASE FOR EUROPEAN EXCEPTIONALISM

Reportage – the evidence

The first chapter of this book set out the parameters of faith in modern Europe, indicating the principal forms of religion that exist in the different parts of the continent. These were presented as a range of variations on a discernible theme – namely relatively low levels of religious practice and credal assent, alongside higher levels of both residual attachment and nominal belief. In the initial paragraphs of this section the same question will be tackled from a different perspective, i.e. one that looks at Europe from the outside rather than from within. The subject matter is similarly reversed: instead of setting out what the patterns of European religion are, an attempt will be made to underline what they are *not*, taking each of the preceding case studies as a particular point of reference.

Such patterns do not, first of all, constitute a religious market in the sense that this exists in the United States. Indeed, if the economic analogy be extended, the historic churches in Europe are considerably closer to the notion of public utility than they

European churches public utilities
rather than religious markets

are to a competitive firm. In other words, they will be there when the population has need of them, but do not require overt commitment in the meantime. This was the central theme of Chapters One and Two and carried with it the warning that patterns of religion which flourish in the United States cannot simply be transferred to Europe at will. Europeans who are dissatisfied with their churches do not, on the whole, seek new allegiances (as they might in a market); they remain, very largely, as passive members of their majority churches – reactivating their commitment at pivotal moments in their individual or collective lives.

In terms of the material on Latin America, we discover that Europe, and more especially West Europe, is not a part of the world where Pentecostalism exists as a widespread and popular movement. That is not to say that it doesn't exist at all; it is in fact one of the few parts of the European Church that is growing. But the movement, whether inside or outside the mainstream churches, remains relatively restricted; there is nothing comparable to the dramatic increase in Pentecostalism that we saw in Latin America (or indeed in Africa or the Pacific Rim). Why not was crucial to the argument of Chapter Three.

The Africa chapter posed a similar if not identical question. It introduced the notion of 'reversed mission', an idea that embodies a considerable degree of self-questioning with respect to the relationship between Europe or European churches and their African counterparts. Just which ones are to be senders and which the receivers in the twenty-first century? There can be little doubt that the religious traffic now moves in both directions. So far, however, the in-comers to Europe have, for the most part, established their churches 'on the edge'. Europeans see these as African churches for African people. A major question mark lies over their ability to penetrate further into Europe (both in a geographical and cultural sense). The debate overlaps that presented in the Latin American chapter in so far as the churches in question are frequently Pentecostal in nature.

The forms of religion discovered in the Philippines offer a different contrast. Here both the particular nature of Catholicism and the recent Pentecostal growth, not to mention the important role played by the churches in recent political crises, indicates a degree and intensity in religious life rarely experienced in Europe and at all levels of society. This holds up despite indicators of modernisation, albeit of a very uneven nature. In South Korea, finally, it is almost as if the assumed European trajectory is turned on its head. Here unbelievably rapid modernisation is accompanied by an equally extraordinary surge in the nation's religious life. Both Christianity and Buddhism grew exponentially from the 1960s on. It is only at the turn of the millennium that the indicators falter, provoking yet another set of sociological questions.

Two points are immediately apparent from this overview. First the European observer (whether he or she is a member of one of Europe's churches or simply a spectator) is forced to admit that the familiar is not necessarily the norm in global terms. The assumption that this might be so has been radically shaken by the material presented in the case studies (a principal aim of this book). A second point is, however, equally important – that is to avoid jumping to conclusions in terms of value judgements. It may indeed be the case that patterns of religion in Europe are different from those discovered elsewhere in the Christian world, but it does not follow that they are either better or worse; they are simply different. Indeed opinions will vary enormously in this respect. For some Europeans, what we experience in this part of the world is reassuringly familiar (there is no real need for change); for others, such changes should be positively resisted (European patterns are to be preserved at all costs); and for a third group, both attitudes are a source of great frustration (there is longing for change and an impatience with those who resist this). All three groups, however, are faced with essentially the same question: how do we *explain* the differences that we have established?

Given the material presented in the preceding chapters it is hardly possible to argue that religion, and more specifically Christian religion, is incompatible with modernity, even in its advanced forms. Both in the United States and in South Korea – if not in every case that we have covered – the economic indicators are some of the highest in the world, yet the religious indices are equally impressive. What is it, then, about the European case that leads to a different outcome?

The specificities of European history, economic, political and cultural, provide the starting point. In most of Western Europe, for example, what has become known as the modernisation process took place both relatively early and relatively slowly. Clearly there are huge variations across the continent (from the early days of industrialisation in eighteenth-century Britain to the artificially held back and far more rapid changes in Spain and Portugal following the collapse of the dictatorships), but – by and large – the process has moved through a discernible sequence, i.e. from incipient industrialism, through the dominance of heavy industries and their associated cities to the forms of society known as late or post-modernity (associated with a *post*-industrial economy). All three stages are important if the present situation is to be properly understood.

In the final chapter of *Religion in Modern Britain* (1994), I looked in some detail at each phase in this complex evolution together with their implications for religious people and religious organisations. A major aim of the chapter was to point out that each shift offers advantages and disadvantages for the churches, but that certain types of church organisation will have more difficulty than others in coming to terms with particular stages in the process. Crucial in this respect is the manner in which the institution in question is embedded in its host society. Europe's historic churches offer an obvious illustration. They fitted easily (one could almost say seamlessly) into the patterns of *pre*-industrial society, a hierarchical model which embodied at almost every level the collusions of religion and power derivative of Europe's ecclesiastical history (a pattern that was centuries old). It was hardly surprising, therefore, that these territorially based institutions had a particularly hard time adapting to the major movements of population that took place as European societies not only industrialised, but urbanised. A major dislocation took place at this time from which the historic churches have never fully recovered, in the sense of regaining a significant element of social control over the populations of which they were part.[1] Secularisation theorists have focused a great deal of their argument on this issue, and rightly so.

Alternative ideologies emerged, moreover, to take the place of church teaching – ways of thinking associated both directly and indirectly with the European enlightenment. No longer were the certainties of Christian theology taken for granted. The manner in which they were challenged varied, however, in different parts of the continent. In the Protestant North, (and more particularly in Scandinavia), a model emerged in which the state Church remained prominent, indeed influential, amidst a largely secularised population. In many respects the habits characteristic of Lutheranism simply transferred themselves to the secular sphere in the forms of a social welfare economy. In Latin Europe, in contrast, the confrontation between the Catholic Church and the advocates of the enlightenment became heavily politicised, a conflict which lasted for several generations. One result in this part of Europe was the emergence of a parallel 'church' in the form of the apparatus of a secular state – i.e. an institution equivalent to the Catholic Church, which both transmitted and embodied the alternative, enlightenment ideology.

In terms of the argument so far, the United States is both similar and different. It is similar in the sense that the economy moves through the stages already described. At the industrialising stage, for instance, American cities grew around particular in-

---

dustries just as this happened in Europe (Detroit is an excellent example). Totally different, however, were the capacities of the churches (in the plural) to move with the industrial process rather than to resist this. New and adaptable forms of church life became in fact part and parcel of the changes taking place, as wave after wave of immigrants to nineteenth- and twentieth-century America brought with them diverse forms of religion already uprooted from their European (sometimes parochial) origins. It was these innovative forms of religion that embedded themselves vertically rather than horizontally into American society (see Chapter Two), permitting far greater flexibility as the economy developed.[2]

In America, furthermore, there is an entirely different relationship with enlightenment ideas. The assumed confrontations of European society (particularly in its Latin forms) are very largely left behind. Indeed Bouretz (forthcoming) argues that the American version of the enlightenment in many ways embodies the best of both Protestant (more specifically German) and Catholic (French) models. In the United States *both* the positive nature of religion *and* the freedom to believe (or indeed not to) are defended. The separation of Church and State ensures, moreover, that these affirmations do not become confused with the political sphere. Hence an entirely different configuration in the new world: nation building and economic development become associated with religious vitality within which appropriate elements of the enlightenment thinking are encouraged rather than resisted – a virtuous circle is brought into being, quite different from the dislocations and downward spirals experienced in Europe.

The specificities of the American case, not least of the American enlightenment, could be developed at considerable length, drawing from a substantial scholarly literature.[3] At this point, however, a second set of comparisons needs to be established, concentrating this time on the chapters which describe developing rather than the developed economies. South Korea

The American enlightenment

has been the most successful of these; here a dramatic and lasting transformation has been wrought, a pre-modern society has become an Asian tiger. The Latin American examples are somewhat different but have a good deal in common with the Philippino case: in both economic development has indeed occurred but has been extremely uneven, leading to dramatic differences in prosperity both within as well as between populations. In both places, moreover (as indeed in Korea), the growth of the mega-city has outstripped anything experienced at the time of the industrial revolution in Europe (or indeed in the United States). It is almost as if these economies have leapt from a pre-industrial phase to a post-industrial one, vastly increasing the tensions that accompany more gradual economic and social change. The African case is different again. As we have seen, with the exception of South Africa, the economic situation in this continent gives continuing cause for concern in that many of the indicators fall rather than rise, exposing huge numbers of people to at best a marginal existence. The ravages of AIDS in large parts of Africa have made a desperate situation even worse.

It is in these situations that Pentecostalism seems to gain a purchase. The many and different forms of Pentecostal religion that can be found in the developing world have a common feature in this respect; they create havens in which both individuals and groups find the strength to cope with the vicissitudes of both economic and political uncertainty.[4] Pentecostalism has succeeded in this respect, when so many other attempts have failed (various forms of community action, for example). Such success demands attention; at its best it is deeply impressive. The very success of Pentecostalism in the developing world may, however, offer a clue to why it does less well in Europe (in addition that is to the reasons addressed in Chapter Three). Quite simply, the spaces that Pentecostalism inhabits so effectively on a global canvas do not exist in Europe (at least not to the same extent), unsurprisingly given the very different economic

Europe: The Exceptional Case

The openings for P. don't exist
in Europe, where secular alternatives are present

trajectory in this part of the world. It is the same trajectory, moreover, that accounts for the greater development of secular alternatives in Europe – both cultural and institutional.

The preceding account is skeletal.[5] It has been offered in order to reveal the multiplicity of factors (economic, political, cultural and ecclesiological) that must be taken into account in understanding not only the particular nature of European religion, but the dangers that will arise if this case is used as the basis of generalisation. Nor, more importantly, is it possible to generalise from sociological approaches (i.e. strong versions of secularisation theory), which to a large extent are part and parcel of the same process, not least in their connections with European forms of the enlightenment. How then should the sociologist proceed in understanding the huge variety of cases that exist in the modern world? That is the question to be tackled in the second section of this chapter. Before doing so, however, two more immediate tasks require attention: the first relates to the remaining categories in the Runciman scheme; the second concerns the changes that might be possible *within* the specificities of the European case. To say that European patterns of religion are exceptional in global terms is not the same as saying that they are immutable.

Runciman elaborated four distinct sociological tasks (see Chapter Two). So far in this chapter, we have dealt with two of these – reportage and explanation. It is important to grasp that the two that remain – description (in the sense of what it 'feels' like to be part of a particular situation) and evaluation or policy-making – also resonate within the framework of European exceptionalism. In terms of the former, for example, it is clear that European reactions to being religious are, like everything else, peculiarly European. Europeans who are actively religious become used to being a minority. They are prone, in consequence, to consider themselves outside the mainstream of their respective societies – a tendency reciprocated, to a considerable extent, by the mainstream itself (a milieu in which the chattering classes and the media are disproportionately present). Hence

European Christians feel they
are outside the mainstream - +
hide their fact

two interrelated characteristics: not only do believing Europeans become somewhat defensive in their reactions, they frequently attempt in everyday life to conceal the labels that the actively religious in other parts of the world claim with pride (a very noticeable difference in religious behaviour once it is pointed out).[6]

On a superficial level, this is undoubtedly true of European society. At a deeper level, however, something rather more complex may be going on, an ambiguity nicely illustrated by the following episode. In 2000 (the millennial year) the National Gallery in London mounted an exhibition entitled 'Seeing Salvation'. The exhibition was not large but contained a carefully selected set of European paintings and sculpture depicting the story of the passion. (In itself it was a powerful indicator of Europe's religious past in cultural as well as religious terms.) The theme was unashamedly Christian. To the surprise of everyone, including the staff of the gallery, the exhibition was extraordinarily popular and drew unprecedented numbers. It also provoked a considerable correspondence addressed to the Director of the gallery, a correspondence that I have been privileged to read.[7]

With reference to the argument of this section, two contradictory themes emerge from these letters. The first endorses the marginality of religion to the mainstream of British life in so far as numerous writers congratulate the Director on his *courage* in mounting an explicitly Christian exhibition in order to celebrate the millennium. It is here that we find evidence in favour of the secularisation of the British mainstream – why else would the Director require courage to act in this way? Conversely, the sheer pleasure that the exhibition gave to so many people (again a dominant theme in the correspondence), alongside the very large numbers of people who attended, conveys a rather different story: namely that the supposed secularisation, or even secularism, of British society might not be as deeply rooted as it first

Europe: The Exceptional Case

Reactions to 'seeing salvation'

appears. The realities that lie beneath the veneer are considerably more complex. They reflect, in fact, a point underlined in previous chapters (pp. 4, 46) – namely that Europeans may indeed be aware that the 'keystone' of the arch of European values is crumbling, but they are not altogether complacent about this situation. Probing these complexities further requires innovative sociological techniques, not least those that are associated with subjective as well as objective attributes. It is a way of thinking developed further in *Religion in Modern Europe* (Davie 2000a).

Contextually insensitive policy-making, finally, is unlikely to be effective, a point made forcibly in Chapter Two. With this in mind, attempts to 'copy' situations or solutions that work well in other parts of the world should be resisted unless there is a very good reason to do otherwise; they are likely to have un-anticipated (quite possibly negative) consequences in the Euro-pean context. Rather more creative is an approach that takes into account the possibility that European patterns of religion may themselves be undergoing change. European ways of doing things may well be distinct but they continue to evolve, and in so doing they are responding to external as well as internal stimuli. It is at this point, moreover, that the preceding case studies begin to resonate.

From obligation to consumption: the changing nature of European religion[8]

At the start of the twentieth century, a whole set of interrelated shifts are occurring in the religious life of Europe. First the historic churches – despite their continuing presence – are sys-tematically losing their capacity to discipline the religious thinking of large sections of the population, especially amongst the young. That is abundantly clear. The latter respond, however, in complex ways – they are just as ready to experiment with new forms of belief as they are to reject the notion of belief altogether, a tendency that is (or appears to be) inversely related

From obligation to consumption
in Europe

to the capacities of the churches to exert control (see Chapter One). At the same time, the range of choice is becoming wider as innovative forms of religion come into Europe from outside, largely as the result of the movement of people (a major theme of the preceding chapters). Populations that have arrived in Europe primarily for economic reasons bring with them different ways of being religious, some Christian and some not. And quite apart from the incoming movements, European people travel the world, experiencing amongst other things considerable religious diversity. In this sense a genuine religious market is emerging in most parts of the continent.

The crucial question lies, however, not in the existence of the market in itself but in the capacities of Europeans to make use of this, the major point of contrast with the United States. Having underlined this difference many times, I am not about to change my mind. I *am*, however, beginning to wonder whether a significant and this time authentically European mutation might be taking place, both inside and outside the historic churches. The mutation in question takes the form of a gradual shift away from an understanding of religion as an obligation and towards an increasing emphasis on consumption. In other words, what until moderately recently was simply imposed (with all the negative connotations of this word), or inherited (a rather more positive spin) becomes instead a matter of personal choice. I go to church (or to another religious organisation) because I want to, maybe for a short period or maybe for longer, to fulfil a particular rather than a general need in my life and where I will continue my attachment so long as it provides what I want, but I have no *obligation* either to attend in the first place or to continue if I don't want to.

If (and the question must remain tentative) such a shift is indeed taking place, what might be the implications for the patterns of religion in modern Europe? The first point to grasp, paradoxically, is that the emergent pattern is not only entirely compatible with vicariousness but to a large extent depends

Vicariousness

upon it: the churches need to be there in order that individuals may attend them if they so choose. The chemistry, however, gradually alters, a shift which is discernible in both practice and belief, not to mention the connections between them. An obvious illustration of this process can be found in the patterns of confirmation in the Church of England. It is true that the overall numbers of confirmations have dropped dramatically in the post-war period, evidence once again of institutional decline. In England, though not yet in the Nordic countries, confirmation is no longer a teenage rite of passage (imposed by the institution), but a relatively rare event undertaken as a matter of personal choice by people of all ages. Hence the marked rise in the proportion of adult confirmations amongst the candidates overall – up to 40 per cent by the mid 1990s (by no means enough, however, to offset the fall among teenagers).

Confirmation becomes, therefore, a very significant event for those individuals who choose this option, an attitude that is bound to affect the rite itself – which now includes the space for a public declaration of faith. It becomes in fact an opportunity to make public what has often been an entirely private activity (see below). It is increasingly common, moreover, to baptise an adult candidate immediately before the confirmation, a gesture which is evidence in itself of the fall in infant baptism some twenty to thirty years earlier. Taken together, these events indicate a marked change in the nature of membership in the historic churches which become, in some senses, much more like their non-established counterparts. Voluntarism (in some senses a market) is beginning to establish itself de facto, regardless of the constitutional position of the institution in question. Or to continue the chemical analogy a little further, a whole set of new reactions are set off which in the *longer* term (the stress is important) may have a profound effect on the nature of European religion.

One final remark concludes this section. It concerns the public

---

Conceptual Maps   149

as well as the private implications of 'choosing' religion. Classic versions of secularisation theory (not least Bruce 1996, 1999) carry with them the notion that chosen religion is necessarily privatised religion. It is an indication that the sacred canopy that used to embrace the totality of believers is no longer operative; religion has become instead simply a matter of life-style and personal preference. Prompted by discussions with sociologists in the Nordic countries,[9] I am no longer convinced that this is so. Those who opt seriously for religion in European societies will want to make their views heard in public as well as private debate. It is at this point, moreover, that the forms of religion (both Christian and non-Christian) that have arrived more recently within Europe begin to make an effective impact: they offer positive (at times inspirational) models to the host community – the learning process is running in both directions.

THEORETICAL RESOURCES

A case has been made for European exceptionalism, indicating at least some of the implications that this might have for the ongoing life of Europe's churches, which themselves continue to evolve. Looking at Europe from the outside proved to be a useful exercise in this respect: patterns of religion in Europe may well be distinct from those in the rest of the world, but they are by no means immune from them – unsurprisingly given that the possibilities for exchange (both of people and approaches) are increasing all the time. But what, exactly, is Europe distinct from (is it one thing or many) and can such differences be conceptualised in theoretical as well as empirical (i.e. case study) terms? It is these questions and the tools that are required for their understanding that are central to the following discussion.

A number of theoretical approaches have already been alluded to. In Chapter One, for example, the emphasis lay on secularis-ation theory, stressing the essentially European origins of this

European secularization / American rational
choice theory

approach, a theme that re-emerged in the earlier part of
this chapter. Chapter Two contained an outline of what might — *the*
be called the American equivalent, rational choice theory, once *only*
again a mode of theorising which has emerged from a specific *altern-*
context. In both cases the somewhat bounded nature of these *ative?*
approaches became apparent, especially in their stronger, more
dogmatic forms. In terms of the Latin American material, for
example, it was only the more flexible versions of secularisation
theory that permitted the insights necessary for understanding
the emergence of Pentecostalism – those in other words that paid
attention to contingent variables and the likelihood that different
patterns will emerge in different parts of the world.

The need for sensitivity in this respect has been illustrated
with reference to geographical rather than conceptual maps. In
geographical terms, the point is immediately obvious: maps of
the Alps cannot simply be transferred to the Rockies or the
Andes (or vice versa) without serious consequences. The corol-
lary to underline at this point is that using the wrong *conceptual*
map is just as misleading (dangerous even) as using the wrong
geographical map, and in more than one respect. Not only do
such maps indicate inappropriate routes, they are equally likely
to *distract* the researcher from the features that do require attention. The inability of numerous scholars even to acknowledge
the presence of Pentecostalism (in its early days), never mind to
study the phenomenon seriously, is a case in point.

All analogies are dangerous if they are pushed too far. It might
none the less be helpful to consider a rather different sort of
map in terms of the understanding of religion (in this case
Christianity) in the modern world. Such maps would start from
a different perspective. Instead of looking at the European or
the American case, and trying to decide which if any was typical,
or conversely exceptional, the emphasis would lie in creating an
unspecific map of 'mountains' that can be adapted to each and
every case.[10] Are there, in other words, sufficient features in
common for the different patterns or trajectories of Christianity

to be placed on one map (albeit with significant variations), or must we begin afresh each time?

The understandings of both modernity and the process of modernisation can be considered in these terms. They revolve around the notion that a core concept or process can be identified, applicable – with a certain number of adaptations – to the multiplicity of examples that are to be found in the real world. The literature in this field is immense and goes back to the founding fathers of sociology – not least to Marx himself, whose insights into the nature and consequences of industrialism remain required reading even if his more specific prophecies were seriously mistaken. In this chapter, the discussion will be far more modest: it will concentrate primarily on the relationship between modernisation and secularisation. Are the two necessarily connected and in what ways? Or to put the same question in terms of the 'map' analogy: is the decrease of religion, or more modestly of certain forms of religion, a necessary feature of modern landscape (i.e. intrinsic to the modernisation process) or simply a contingent one (i.e. extrinsic, in the sense that it will be there in some cases but not in others)?

Two studies (or groups of studies) offer contrasting routes into the discussion. The first concerns the empirical testing of some aspects of the modernisation theory using data from the World Values Survey of which the European material employed in Chapter One formed the first part – bringing the argument of the book as a whole nicely full circle. The principal source of material for the World Surveys lies in the work of Ronald Ingelhart and his team in the University of Michigan.[11] The second approach is primarily theoretical; it is directed by Shmuel Eisenstadt from the Hebrew University in Jerusalem, but draws from a wide range of comparative cases embracing, once again, examples from almost all global regions (and indeed almost all world faiths). Eisenstadt's thinking embodies an innovative concept – that of 'multiple modernities'. In other words it moves sharply away from a single or core understanding of

really 'multiple modernities'

either modernity or the modernisation process. The case studies together with the comparative frame have been published in two dedicated issues of *Daedalus* (the journal of the American Academy of Arts and Sciences).[12]

Testing modernisation theory

Modernisation theory evokes strong reactions and has become, more often than not, heavily ideological. In the immediate post-war period, for example, there were those who considered it both necessary and appropriate to bring 'modern' ways of doing things to the developing societies of the world. Such policies rested on attitudes, often well intentioned, which assumed that traditional values necessarily prevent the proper course of modernisation (i.e. effective and inevitable capitalist development); it was right therefore that they be replaced. Such views were vehemently opposed, two decades later, by those (mostly dependency theorists) who saw the lack of modernisation of large parts of the world in an entirely different light. It had nothing to do with the value systems of local populations and everything to do with the greed of advanced capitalist societies. The inequalities of the global economy were the outcomes not of 'backward' values but of capitalist exploitation. Unsurprisingly, this too has been criticised by those who perceive advantages as well as disadvantages in capitalist investment on a global scale and not solely for the elite.

Embedded in critique and counter-critique are different understandings of the modernisation process. On the one hand there are those who maintain 'that economic development is linked with coherent and, to some extent, predictable changes in culture and social and political life' (Inglehart and Baker 2000: 21).[13] On the other are scholars (mostly dependency theorists and cultural relativists) who reject such a possibility – the relationship between the two sets of variables is essentially random. Data from the World Values Survey (the focus of this section) are strongly supportive of the former view, but with important modifications to earlier versions of the theory (Inglehart 1997, Ingelhart and Baker 2000).

There are, first of all, two stages to bear in mind in the ongoing process of modernisation: the first occurs when societies move from a pre-industrial to industrial economy and the second as the economy begins to mutate once again – this time to a service-based, post-industrial mode of organisation. At each stage, moreover, there is an associated shift in the value-systems espoused by the populations in question but not always in the direction anticipated by the early theorists of modernisation. It becomes increasingly clear, for example, that it is no longer possible to assume a linear evolution in the development of modern societies, i.e. towards an increasingly technical, mechanical, rationalised, bureaucratic, and indeed secular environment in which the values associated with economic and physical security become paramount. Something very different was taking place in many parts of the world. More precisely: as economies moved from the industrial to the post-industrial phase, the populations in question began to place far more stress on *post*-materialist values, not least an increasing emphasis on well-being and the quality of life – i.e. something rather more subtle than simple survival.

We return once again to the questions (i.e. the long-term evolution of industrial economies) that preoccupied me in the last chapter of *Religion in Modern Britain*. In the earlier sections of the present discussion (p. 141–2) the stress lay on the shift from pre-industrial to industrial societies and the different effects that this had in Europe and the new world. At *this* point, it is the movement away from industrial society and into new forms of economic and social life that resonates most strongly. The data from the World Values Survey firmly endorse the latter shift: across a wide variety of societies, West Europe included, a rather different configuration emerges as industrial economies mutate into post-industrial ones, i.e. into societies characterised by growing rather than declining evidence of spiritual concern (indeed of religious belief), though not, it is clear, of institutional commitment. Here, moreover, is further support for the possibility that European patterns of religion (just like any others) will continue to develop: West Europe may be distinctive but it is by no means static.

So much for the longitudinal sequence. Ingelhart (1997) and Inglehart and Baker (2000) then introduce a second but equally important dimension in the argument, namely the diversity between nations, or groups of nations. Drawing from the huge data sets of the World Values Survey, it becomes increasingly clear that different societies follow different trajectories even when they are subject to the same forces of economic development. This is a both/and situation. On the one hand the rise of industrial society and its subsequent mutation into post-industrial forms are associated with coherent and empirically discernible cultural shifts. On the other, the systems which emerge at each stage in this evolution are path dependent: more precisely they reflect Protestant, Catholic, Islamic or Confucian backgrounds, each of which display distinctive value systems. The associated differences, shaped very largely by the cultural (and more specifically religious) heritage in question, persist even after controlling for the effects of economic development. Hence the following conclusion:

> Economic development tends to push societies in a common direction, but rather than converging, they seem to move on parallel trajectories, shaped by their cultural heritages. We doubt that the forces of modernization will produce a homogenized world culture in the foreseeable future. (Inglehart and Baker 2000: 49)

In terms of the case studies described in this book, the patterns or maps that emerge are satisfying if not quite 'perfect' (Inglehart 1997: 335). There is evidence, first of all, of Europe's comparative secularity. Both parts of West Europe (North and South), for example, score noticeably higher on the secular-rational scale than the United States, the Latin American countries, the Philippines and the African examples. (The South Korean case is rather more ambiguous, though the movement of South Korea in terms of economic development between 1981 and 1990 can be clearly seen.) Cutting across these axes, however, lies a second set of contrasts: those between primarily Catholic and primarily Protestant cultures. It is at this point, moreover, that the affinities between Northern Europe and North America reveal themselves, with Canada edging closer to the European pattern all the time. Latin America (including the Philippines) links itself to Latin Europe. There is, finally, a hint that the 'lead' societies in the modern world are more likely to be those of Northern Europe than the United States, a crucial but contentious point that will be immediately challenged in the following section.[14]

Multiple modernities

The work on multiple modernities embodies a rather different approach, in that it confronts the notion of global convergence in theoretical rather than empirical terms. The *negative* agenda is unequivocally set in the following paragraph:

> The notion of 'multiple modernities' denotes a certain view of the contemporary world – indeed of the history and characteristics of the modern era – that goes against the views long prevalent in scholarly and general discourse. It goes against the view of the 'classical' theories of modernization and of the convergence of industrial societies prevalent in the 1950s, and indeed against the classical sociological analyses of Marx, Durkheim, and (to a large extent) even of Weber, at least in one reading of his work. They all assumed, even only implicitly, that the cultural program of modernity as it developed in modern Europe and the basic institutional constellations that emerged there would ultimately take over in

multiple modernities

all modernizing and modern societies; with the expansion of
modernity, they would prevail throughout the world.
(Eisenstadt 2000: 1)

Right from the start, therefore, Eisenstadt challenges both the
assumption that modernising societies are convergent, and the
notion of Europe (or indeed anywhere else) as the lead society
in the modernising process.

How then does the multiple modernities approach develop
from a *positive* point of view? In the introductory essay to the
set of comparative cases, Eisenstadt suggests that the best way to
understand the modern world (in other words to grasp the
history and nature of modernity) is to see this as 'a story of
continual constitution and reconstitution of a multiplicity of cultural programs' (2000: 2). A second point follows from this.
These ongoing reconstitutions do not drop from the sky; they
emerge as the result of endless encounters on the part of both
individuals and groups, all of whom engage in the creation (and
recreation) of both cultural and institutional formations, but
within *different* economic and cultural contexts. Once this way
of thinking is firmly in place it becomes easier to appreciate
one of the fundamental paradoxes of Eisenstadt's writing: namely
that to engage with the Western understanding of modernity, or
even to oppose it, is as indisputably modern as to embrace it.

What then is the authentic core of modernity? The question
becomes, in fact, very difficult to answer in that modernity is
more of an attitude (a distinctive epistemology) than a set of
characteristics. In its early forms, it embodied above all a notion
of the future which was realisable by means of human agency.
As soon as the process was set in motion, however, even the
core of modernity was beset by internal contradictions. Were
such societies to be totalising or pluralistic, for example? Or what
degree of control/autonomy was considered desirable? Hence, to
give an institutional illustration, the very different formulations
of the nation state (an essential feature of modernity) that

emerged even in different parts of Europe – hegemonic in France and the Nordic countries (though differently so in each case) as opposed to the rather more pluralistic pattern adopted in Britain or The Netherlands. Should we be surprised therefore at the even greater transformations that took place (both culturally and institutionally) when the idea of modernity transferred itself to the new world, and then, bit by bit, out of the west altogether? Following Eisenstadt, diversity is simply assumed within the modernising process; it becomes in fact part of modernity itself.[15]

In the World Values Study, the initial emphasis lay on the longitudinal shifts in the modernisation process with the emphasis on diversity following from this. In Eisenstadt's essay, it is almost the other way round in so far as the two can be separated at all. The shifting nature of the modernity (or more accurately modernities) is none the less crucial to Eisenstadt's thinking – a point nicely illustrated in his continuing analysis of the State, this time in late as opposed to early modern societies. Globalisation (in all its diverse forms) has changed dramatically the 'institutional, symbolic, and ideological contours of the modern, national and revolutionary states' (2000: 16). No longer, for example, can these institutions adequately control much of modern living, whether in economic, political or cultural terms. Despite technologically developed means of restraint, the flows and counter-flows of modern living increasingly transcend political boundaries. The construction of multiple modernities continues none the less (that is its nature), but in constantly changing circumstances.

Central to this process in recent decades is the appearance of new actors and new entities, among them a whole range of social movements, who assume responsibility for the emergent problems of the modern world. Feminist or ecological organisations (often transnational in nature) provide excellent examples, but so too do religious movements – even those commonly known as fundamentalist. It is true that the latter are vehemently opposed to the west and to the ideologies embodied therein. Fundamen-

Europe: The Exceptional Case

talist movements are, however, quintessentially modern in the manner in which they set their goals and in the means that they adopt to achieve them: their outlooks, for example, are truly global and their technologies highly developed. Just like their secular counterparts, they are redefining and reconstituting the concept of modernity, but in their own terms.[16]

With respect to this chapter as a whole, the crucial point to emerge from Eisenstadt's work is the continued space for religion and for religious movements within the unfolding interpretations of modernity. The forms of religion, moreover, may be as diverse as the forms of modernity. Indeed the examples that follow in the special issue of *Daedalus* offer Christian, Muslim, Hindu and Confucian illustrations, but regrettably no discussion of Pentecostalism. The author of one of these, Nilufer Göle, concludes that the essential core of modernity resides in its potential for self-correction, a capacity that by definition must be ongoing given that the problems that preoccupy us at the start of the twenty-first century could not even be imagined in the early stages of modernisation. Thus religion (in Göle's essay this is innovative forms of Islam) becomes one resource among many in the process of continual self-correction. More precisely, 'modernity is not simply rejected or readopted but critically and creatively re-appropriated by new religious discursive and social practices in non-Western contexts' (Göle 2000: 93).

Two points bring this discussion to a close. First, to underline once again that European versions of modernity are indeed distinct (most notably in their comparative secularity), a possibility underpinned by theoretical as well as empirical considerations. But, second, they are not distinct from a single undifferentiated other. They are simply one modernity among many in the modern world and, like all the others, in the process of continual reconstruction.

modernity = potential for self-correction
& religious change is part of it — & so is
European secularity

G. D's 'exercise in humility'

CONCLUDING REMARKS

How then should the European respond? What lessons if any can be learnt from these pages? In answering these questions, I will simply speak for myself. For me the writing of this book has been an exercise in humility. If Europe is not the global prototype, both Europe and Europeans have everything to learn from cases other than their own. Not least among such lessons is the importance of taking the religious factor seriously, and in public as well as private life. Taking religion seriously, moreover, is greatly facilitated by the assumption that you expect it to be there, as an integral, *normal* part of modern as well as modernising societies.

In many respects, the aftermath of the cataclysmic events of 11 September 2001 reveals just how far short Europeans fall from achieving this goal. Since the attack on the Twin Towers, for example, the debate about religion has veered too often from vilification to trivialisation, indicating not only the difficulty of accepting the normality of the concept, but (even more importantly) the lack of a shared vocabulary with which to discuss the emergent issues – a point that could be repeated with reference to a host of further, if thankfully less catastrophic, examples. One will suffice. Lynas (2001) provides a fascinating insider account of the attempts to include a religious or spiritual component in the ill-fated Millennium Dome. Whilst it is clear that almost everyone thought this was a good idea in principle (though disagreed sharply about its contents), very few possessed the conceptual understanding necessary to put such ideas into practice.

One way of initiating the learning process is, surely, to spend time with those who are arriving in Europe almost on a daily basis. In this respect, listening is the first priority (an exercise in welcome in itself). In terms of policy-making, in contrast, a considerable degree of discernment will be necessary, for not

Europe: The Exceptional Case

learning lessons from immigrant-

everything that comes in from outside will be appropriate (or indeed welcome) in the European context. Deciding what to accept and what to reject will be a demanding process, requiring sensitive as well as informed decision-making – in the secular as well as the religious sphere.

Finally writing this book has become for me an exercise in what it means to be modern. I conclude that it is as modern to draw from the resources of religion in order to critique the secular as it is to draw from the secular in order to critique the religious. Only in Europe has the equation become seriously imbalanced. Or to put the same point in rather more abstract terms, secularisation is essentially a European phenomenon and is extrinsic rather than intrinsic to the modernising process per se.

NOTES

Chapter 1: SETTING THE SCENE: THE PARAMETERS OF FAITH IN MODERN EUROPE

1. Note, however, the case of the English-speaking Dominions who, initially at least, modelled their arrangements on Europe.
2. The European Values Study is a major cross-national survey of human values, first carried out in Europe in 1981 and then extended to other countries worldwide. It was designed by the European Values Systems Study Group (EVSSG). Analyses of the 1981 material can be found in Harding and Phillips, with Fogarty (1986) and in Stoetzel (1983). A restudy took place in 1990. Published material from this can be found in Timms (1992), Ashford and Timms (1992), Barker, Halman and Vloet (1992) and Ester, Halman and de Moor (1994). Barker *et al.* includes a useful bibliography of the whole enterprise up to 1992. A further restudy took place in 1999/2000, from which the initial results are now available (Halman 2001). Up-to-date information about the survey and the data that have emerged from it can be found on the following website: http://evs.kub.nl. The longitudinal aspects of the study enhance the data considerably.
3. See, for example, the parallel study on Religion and Moral Pluralism, directed by Wolfgang Jagodzinski from the Institute for Applied Social Research in the University of Cologne.
4. For a fuller picture of these data – essential for any detailed work – see Stoetzel (1983), Harding, Phillips with Fogarty (1986), Barker, Halman and Vloet (1992), Ester, Halman and de Moor (1994), and Halman and Riis (1999), together with the individual analyses for each European country involved in the survey.
5. Most striking of all are the *growing* numbers of young people (especially in Northern Europe) who believe both in life after death and in a 'God within' – i.e. in an immanent rather than transcendent God.
6. Information (including statistics) about the Jewish communities in West Europe can be found in Wasserstein (1996) and Webber (1994).
7. Estimates of the size of Europe's Muslim population are, inevitably, related to questions about immigration. Statistics relating to illegal immigration are particularly problematic. See Nielsen (1995: 170–1) for a discussion of the statistical question and related difficulties.
8. The full title is the Centro Studi sulle Nuove Religioni. Information about CESNUR is most easily accessed via www.cesnur.org, an impressive, very up to date and multilingual website.
9. The competing ideology is known in France as *laïcité*, a word that is almost

impossible to translate into English. Strictly speaking it refers to the absence of religion from the public sphere. At times, however, the connotations have been considerably more negative.

10. A number of cases concerning intolerance of minorities in Greece have been brought, successfully, to the European courts. An excellent source of information on the detail of these cases can be found on the CESNUR website (see note 8).

11. Exactly when and why these changes were initiated is subject to debate amongst historians; starting dates vary considerably from place to place.

12. Precisely the same point has been made by Robert Putnam with reference to his work on voluntary organisations in the United States (Putnam 2000). See Chapter Two for a fuller discussion of this.

Chapter 2: AMERICAN ACTIVITY: A VIBRANT RELIGIOUS MARKET

1. The 1998 Hadaway, Marler and Chaves' article forms part of a 'Symposium on Church Attendance' in the United States published by the *American Sociological Review.* The controversy was sparked by their 1993 article. The accuracy of these figures (notably the degree to which attendance is overestimated) remains an ongoing controversy in American sociology, with opinions quite sharply divided.

2. It is true that in Europe, as well as in the United States, growth is found in the more conservative, often evangelical groups, both within the mainstream denominations and outside them. Such growth, however, is insufficient to compensate for the losses sustained in more liberal groups.

3. A partial exception can perhaps be found in Poland, where the traditional disciplines still operate at least in rural areas (much less so in the cities).

4. Interestingly in Sweden, both the formal, or nominal, membership of the churches and that of the trade unions has remained high (they are, moreover, spoken of in very similar ways). Active membership of either is, of course, a very different matter.

5. The crucial point is the following: Americans still go bowling but no longer do this in organised leagues. Social capital is generated by the interaction between team members, not by the activity of bowling itself.

6. It is important to remember that the applicability of the Putnam thesis to the British case is not universally accepted. Hall (1999), for example, fails to find support for Putnam in the British data.

7. Davie (1994), especially Chapter Five, discusses the British case in some detail.

8. For some faith communities, voluntarism presents particular difficulties. Muslims, for example, think and act entirely differently – for them the notion of a state Church is rather easier than the American model.

9. Some churches in Europe have, of course, responded to this phenomenon; Holy Trinity Brompton is an excellent example.

10. Edgell Becker (1999) offers another good example, describing in considerable

detail congregations that appeal to particular kinds of family, each of them catering for very specific needs.

11. The notion of compensators has proved controversial; it has been dropped in more recent versions of the rational choice theory.

12. Such churches are unable to survive without state subsidy, part of which (following the RC theorists) goes to finance a complacent, not to say lazy, professional class.

13. There is plenty of evidence that Europeans feared that televangelism would penetrate European culture, given the increasing deregulation of the media; in Britain, for example, it became a major preoccupation in parliamentary debate (Quicke and Quicke 1992).

14. Religious minorities in Sweden tend to resent the wealth and power of the Swedish Church. This is less the case in England where a much less wealthy established Church is seen as the protector of all religions – whether Christian or not.

15. Interestingly, the 2001 Scottish census included a more detailed and considerably more effective question.

16. See the subtitle of the recently published collection of papers, edited by Lyon and Van Die (2001), a text which expands the argument of this section.

Chapter 3: LATIN AMERICA: AN EXAMPLE OF GLOBAL PENTECOSTALISM

1. These statistics are, of course, constantly changing; care should be taken in their interpretation. See note 9 for a constantly updated source.

2. A peak appears, however, to have been reached in Guatemala (between a quarter and a third of the population are now Protestant).

3. See note 2. The growth may not go on indefinitely, a conclusion suggested by the South Korea case (Chapter Five) as well as the Guatemalan material.

4. Much of this discussion can be seen in terms of social capital (Chapter Two); for some commentators Pentecostalism generates positive social capital, for others the outcomes are rather more ambiguous. For Levine and Stoll (1997), the discussion of social capital becomes a central theme.

5. This comparison begs an important question. Just what models are helpful in our attempts to understand the forms of Pentecostalism that are spreading through the developing world?

6. The Fundamentalist Project was introduced in Chapter One. Why this chapter is included in such a volume is, however, more problematic in that neither liberation theology, nor Pentecostalism fit easily with the notion of fundamentalism as this is set out in the University of Chicago Project. With respect to Pentecostalism in particular, Bernice Martin (2001) draws attention both to the anomaly itself and to its theoretical, not to say ideological, implications.

7. Woodhead (2002) is an excellent resource on this point.

8. A similar dilemma can be found in the discussion of power: it cannot be right both to condemn power and to encourage empowerment. The latter, if taken seriously, will lead willy-nilly to the latter.

9. See, for example, the bibliography compiled by Corten (1997), or the website maintained by Anthony Gill for the Latin American Studies Program of Providence College (www.providence.edu/las/index.htm).

10. Candomblé came to Brazil with African slaves; it mixes African and Roman Catholic beliefs, a synthesis in which contact with the deceased remains central. Umbanda is also syncretic, but is more affluent and better organised than Candomblé. It contains African, Amerindian and Catholic features, but originated in Brazil rather than in Africa itself.

11. Martin adds an interesting note in this respect. Modern change is increasingly rapid; with this in mind the decline of Pentecostalism could in the fullness of time be as fast as its growth (2001b: 28).

12. Note, however, the collection of articles in Smith and Prokopy (1999), with the proviso that the RCT articles within this collection are in turn critiqued by Löwy (2001).

13. See note 9 for details of this website.

14. The literature of Livets Ord is interesting in this respect. Worship should, above all, be up to date and relevant; in other words the very opposite of a cultural museum.

Chapter 4: AFRICAN INITIATIVES: AN ALTERNATIVE VIEW OF GLOBAL RELIGION

1. The conference was held at New College in Edinburgh in May 1992. It was arranged jointly by the Centre of African Studies and the Centre for the Study of Christianity in the Non-western World.

2. This conference is recognised as the high water mark of the missionary movement from the west to the rest of the world.

3. Exactly the same point is discussed by Sundkler (2000: 91–6); hence the predilection of the author for the term 'transition' rather than 'conversion' for the initial, often corporate, movement of African people to Christianity

4. At least it does in theory. But as Ranger (2000) points out, it doesn't quite deliver in practice.

5. Interestingly, the decisive role of women comes a little later. See, for example, Sundkler (2000: 681) and Ward (1999: 225–6).

6. See also 'On the rationality of conversion', *Africa*, 45, 1975: 219–35 and 373–99.

7. The loss of life, especially in the early days, was enormous as any first-hand account will reveal. Precisely this point produced a notable reaction in the Sarum Lecture on 'African Initiatives'; it was based on the personal cost (large and small) born by numerous missionary families known, directly or indirectly, to the audience.

8. Turner uses the terms 'New Religious Movements' or 'NERMS'. The at times disproportionate attention given to these movements in many ways parallels the attraction of New Religious Movements (NRMs) in Western society for sociologists of religion at about the same time.

9. The aim of this volume was to encourage African scholars to address Africa's

changing religious scene; the aim, however, was only partially achieved in view, once again, of the economic difficulties of many African scholars.

10. *Journal of Religion in Africa*, XXVIII/3, 1998.

11. Hackett makes an interesting methodological point in this connection: scholars of religion in Africa rarely engage the media and scholars of the media seem blind to the significance of religion. Both, therefore, miss this crucial intersection between the public and the private in African life.

12. In this respect, Pentecostals are in many ways imitating the earlier exhortations of Protestant missionaries to avoid back-sliding; the notion of rupture is however even more clear-cut for Pentecostals than it was for their predecessors.

13. Here the parallels with Martin's analysis of the Latin American case are obvious (Chapter Three). The relationship with Martin's ideas becomes, however, rather more equivocal in Gifford's later writing (Gifford 1998).

14. This information was given to me by Maria Jose Fontales Rosada Nunes. No longer do the vast majority of Brazilians call themselves Catholic – the pattern has become much more varied.

15. This area of Amsterdam acquired global notoriety after a plane crashed onto an apartment building inhabited largely by immigrants.

16. The 1960s saw the onset of relatively late but very rapid secularisation in The Netherlands.

17. *International Review of Mission*, LXXXIX/354, July 2000.

Chapter 5: DIASPORA POPULATIONS: CHRISTIAN COMMUNITIES IN THE FAR EAST

1. Such statistics can, of course, be read in a number of ways. Not only does the meeting in the Philippines stand out as the largest (the point to be made in this chapter), in terms of the argument of this book taken as whole, the *relative* success of the European meetings is also important. One-off gatherings in Europe still draw large numbers of young people, despite the sharp fall-off in regular attendance (Davie 2000a).

2. In contrast, the inhabitants of Luzon and Vasaya, Muslim at the time of the Spanish occupation, were systematically Christianised.

3. See also Ileto (1979) which sets festivals such as this one into a wider socio-political context.

4. Such practices, which become amongst other things a form of initiation ceremony for the Morions, derive initially from the penitential exercises of the colonial priests. They are increasingly condemned by the Church because of their alleged brutality and barbarism, but are currently (and paradoxically) on the increase. It is this kind of practice, moreover, that catches the attention of the Western press.

5. Despite the separation of Church and State, the preamble to the new constitution includes an invocation imploring the aid of Divine Providence.

6. EDSA is a shortened form of Epifanio de los Santos Avenue, a major thoroughfare in Metro Manila.

7. Joseph (Erap) Estrada, a former film star, became President in 1998; his six-year term came to a premature end in April 2001.
8. The transformation is visual as well as cultural. The thousands of Christian churches in the major cities of Korea call attention to their presence by placing neon red crosses on their roofs.
9. I am grateful to SungHo Kim for indicating these sources which are reproduced in his own article, as indeed for his help in understanding the Korean situation as a whole (Kim 2002).
10. Korean Protestantism is internally divided. Figures from the *Korean Torch* 1993 suggest the following: 62% Presbyterian (in several denominations), 11% Methodist, 10% Pentecostal, 8% Holiness and 7% Baptist. Presbyterianism is, however, considerably Pentecostalised.
11. The dramatic change in the Buddhist as well as the Christian presence in post-war Korean society merits a study of its own. A useful source can be found in a special issue of the *Korea Journal*, Autumn 1993, vol. 33/3.
12. This was the plan for an indirect Presidential election as a means of consolidating the regime, ignoring the Korean people's hope for direct election.
13. Such ideas are brought together under the heading Minjung theology, a specifically Korean understanding of liberation theology. Koreans, however, would be wary of the term 'liberation' in their anxiety to avoid Marxist connotations of any kind.
14. Some idea of the scale of this undertaking can be gleaned from the multilingual website maintained by the church itself (www.english.fgtv.com). The site also offers an outline history on the church, from its beginnings as a tent mission (working amongst the disadvantaged) to its extraordinary rapid growth in recent decades. The account of course is written by the church itself; it does not constitute a critical analysis.
15. The Chinese case remains extremely difficult to predict; there are signs, however, of considerable religious growth (both Christian and Buddhist) in recent decades. See Tu Weiming (1996).
16. Freston (2001: 65–9) indicates the complexity of this story in which there are many vested interests. Quite clearly there is a need to avoid simple dichotomies.
17. During the recent ethnic troubles in the region, the Melanesian Brothers have provided a safe refuge for those forced out of their homes and their work on the island of Guadalcanal. The Brothers are amongst the few trusted by all sides in the conflict.

Chapter 6: CONCEPTUAL MAPS

1. Most commentators agree that this is a good thing. Exceptions still exist, however – for example in parts of Poland where a high percentage of priests can still exert an effective pastoral discipline on the rural population.
2. Similar and equally innovative forms of religion do, of course, exist in Europe. Their emergence and continuing significance form an essential part

of the historical account. They remain, however, a secondary rather than dominant motif in the European picture taken as a whole.

3. The contrast between Europe and the United States has caught the eye of commentators since de Tocqueville onwards; so too the possibility of American exceptionalism, reformulated, for example, by Lipset (1996).

4. It is here, moreover, that the historical affinities with Methodism and Puritanism are most clearly displayed.

5. It can – indeed should – be supplemented by the developed theoretical account of these issues offered in Martin (2001a).

6. A small but revealing example can be found in American theatre programmes, in which large numbers of the cast unselfconsciously thank God, alongside their families, both for their talents and for the success that they are enjoying.

7. This correspondence was lent to me by the Director. It consists in some 450 letters relating partly to the 'Seeing Salvation' exhibition in the National Gallery and partly to the television programme of the same title. As a response to the television programmes, the number of letters was in line with previous experience; as a response to an exhibition, it was exceptional.

8. A more detailed version of the argument in this section can be found in Davie (forthcoming).

9. My Nordic (more specifically Danish) colleagues are particularly concerned with the influence of Islam in the European context. Privatised Islam makes no sense and the struggle to find appropriate models for Islam in Europe will affect the host society as much as the in-coming communities – a point that echoes a major theme in these lectures.

10. Such an approach reflects the notion of 'ideal-type' first developed by Weber; that is a 'pure' type against which the multiple examples of reality can be measured.

11. The University of Michigan is the centre of a worldwide network in this respect, which can be accessed through the World Values Survey website – wvs.isr.umich.edu.

12. 'Early Modernities', *Daedalus*, 127/3, summer 1998; 'Multiple Modernities', *Daedalus*, 129/1, winter 2000.

13. A second set of questions follows from this position: those that relate to the causal sequence. Do economic changes engender cultural change (the Marxist position) or do cultural values themselves encourage/influence economic endeavour (the Weberian position)? This ongoing debate lies at the heart of social scientific discussion.

14. It is also worth pointing out the position of Japan in the World Values framework; in WVS terms this is a further example of a society which is both highly modern and highly secular.

15. The intrinsic nature of diversity in the modernisation process emerges as much from the volume on 'Early Modernities' as it does from the one on 'Multiple Modernities'.

16. Eisenstadt (1999) offers a fuller discussion of the nature of fundamentalism in the modern world.

LIST OF REFERENCES

Abrams, M., Gerard, D. and Timms, N. (1985) *Values and Social Change in Britain*, Basingstoke, Macmillan.

Adachi, T. (1994) 'The Morion as stranger', in *Review of Indonesian and Malaysian Affairs*, 28/1: 13–34.

Ahern, G. and Davie, G. (1987) *Inner City God: the Nature of Belief in the Inner City*, London, Hodder and Stoughton.

Ammerman, N. (1997) *Congregation and Community*, New Brunswick, NJ, Rutgers University Press.

Ashford, S. and Timms, N. (1992) *What Europe Thinks: a Study of West European Values*, Aldershot, Dartmouth.

Bäckström, A. (1999) *Från statskyrka till fri folkkyrka (From State Church to Free Folk Church)*, Stockholm, Verbum Publisher.

Bäckström, A. and Bromander, J. (1995) *Kyrkobyggnaden och det offentliga rummet*, Uppsala, Svenska Kyrkans Utredningar (contains an English summary).

Baker, D. (1997) 'From pottery to politics: the transformation of Korean Catholicism', in L. Lancaster and R. Payne (eds.), *Religion and Society in Contemporary Korea*, Berkeley, Institute of East Asian Studies, University of California, 127–68.

Barker, D., Halman, L. and Vloet, A. (1992) *The European Values Study 1981–1990: Summary Report* (published by the Gordon Cook Foundation on behalf of the European Values Group).

Barrett, D. (1982) *World Christian Encyclopedia: a Comparative Study of Churches and Religions in the Modern World AD 1900–2000*, Oxford, Oxford University Press.

Barrett, D., Kurian, G. and Johnson, T. (2001) *World Christian Encyclopedia: a Comparative Study of Churches and Religions in the Modern World* (second edition), Oxford, Oxford University Press.

Bastian, J.-P. (1992) 'Les protestantismes latino-américains: un objet à interroger et à construire', *Social Compass*, 39/3: 327–54.

(1994) *Le Protestantisme en Amérique latine: une approche socio-historique*, Geneva, Labor et Fides.

Bastian, J.-P. and Collange, J.-F. (1999) (eds.) *L'Europe à la recherche de son âme*, Geneva, Labor et Fides.

Bellah, R. (1970) *Beyond Belief: Essays on Religion in a Post Traditional World*, New York, Harper and Row.

Berger, P. (1967) *The Sacred Canopy. Elements of a Sociological Theory of Religion*, New York, Doubleday.

(1992) *A Far Glory: the Quest for Faith in an Age of Credulity*, New York, Free Press.

(1999) (ed.) *The Desecularization of the World: Resurgent Religion and World Politics*, Grand Rapids, Eerdmans Publishing Co.

Berger, S. (1982) *Religion in West European Politics*, London, Frank Cass.

Bibby, R. (2000) 'Canada's mythical religious mosaic: some census findings', *Journal for the Scientific Study of Religion*, 39/2: 235–9.

Birman, P. and Pereira Leite, P. (2000) 'Whatever happened to what used to be called the largest Catholic country in the world?', *Daedalus*, 129/2: 271–90.

Bouretz, P. 'Secularity versus Laïcité: a comparative perspective', paper given at an invited seminar on comparative secularity, Berlin (March 2001). Further details about eventual publication available from the Institute on Religion and World Affairs, Boston University.

Brown, C. (2001) *The Death of Christian Britain*, London, Routledge.

Bruce, S. (1988) *The Rise and Fall of the New Christian Right*, Oxford, Oxford University Press.

(1990) *Pray TV: Televangelism in America*, London, Routledge.

(1992) (ed.) *Religion and Modernization*, Oxford, Oxford University Press.

(1996) *From Cathedrals to Cults: Religion in the Modern World*, Oxford, Oxford University Press.

(1999) *Choice and Religion: a Critique of Rational Choice Theory*, Oxford, Oxford University Press.

Bruce, S., Kivisto, P. and Swatos, B. (1995) (eds.) *The Rapture of Politics: the Christian Right as the United States approaches the year 2000*, New Brunswick, NJ, Transaction.

Brusco, E. (1993) 'The reformation of machismo: asceticism and masculinity among Colombian evangelicals', in D. Stoll and V. Garrard-Burnett (eds.), *Rethinking Protestantism in Latin America*, Philadelphia, Temple University Press, 143–58.

Bunting, M. (1996) 'God's Media Image', *The Tablet*, 16 November: 1505–6.

Cameron, H. (2002) 'The Decline of the Church of England as a Local Membership Organization: Predicting the Nature of Civil Society in 2050', in G. Davie, P. Heelas and L. Woodhead, *Predicting Religion: Mainstream and Margins in the West*, London, Routledge.

Cariño, F. (2000) 'What brings people together (or tears them apart) in the global world?', unpublished paper.

Casanova, J. (2001) 'Religion, the new Millennium and globalization', *Sociology of Religion*, 62/4: 415–41.

Chambers, P. (2000) *Factors in Church Growth and Decline*, unpublished Ph.D. thesis, University of Wales.

Clark, D. (1997) 'History and religion in modern Korea: the case of Protestant Christianity', in L. Lancaster and R. Payne (eds.), *Religion and Society in Contemporary Korea*, Berkeley, Institute of East Asian Studies, University of California, 169–214.

Clarke, P. (1998) (ed.) *New Trends and Developments in African Religions*, Westport, CT, Greenwood Press.

Coleman, S. (2001) *The Globalization of Charismatic Christianity: Spreading the Gospel of Prosperity*, Cambridge, Cambridge University Press.

Corten, A. (1997) 'The growth of the literature of Afro-American, Latin

American and African Pentecostalism', *Journal of Contemporary Religion*, 12/3: 311–24.

Cox, H. (1996) *Fire from Heaven*, New York, Addison-Wesley.

Cucchiari, S. (1988) 'Adapted for heaven: conversion and culture in western Sicily', *American Ethnologist*, 15: 417–41.

(1991) 'Between shame and sanctification: patriarchy and its transformation in Sicilian Pentecostalism', *American Ethnologist*, 18: 687–707.

Daiber, K.-F. (2000) 'Introduction', *Social Compass*, 47/4: 459–66, Special issue on Religion and Modernity in South Korea.

Dancel, M. (1998) 'African independent churches', in R. Wuthnow (ed.), *The Encyclopedia of Politics and Religion*, London, Routledge.

Davie, G. (1994) *Religion in Britain since 1945: Believing without Belonging*, Oxford, Blackwell.

(2000a) *Religion in Modern Europe: a Memory Mutates*, Oxford, Oxford University Press.

(2000b) 'Religion in Britain: changing sociological assumptions', *Sociology*, 34/1: 113–28.

(forthcoming) 'From obligation to consumption: patterns of religion in Northern Europe', paper given at an invited seminar on comparative secularity, Berlin (March 2001). Further details about eventual publication available from the Institute on Religion and World Affairs, Boston University.

'DAWN Research Report' (1991) Prepared by Philippines Crusades Research (5 November).

Defois, G. and Tincq, H. (1997) *Les Médias et l'Eglise*, Paris, CEPJ.

Droogers, A. (1998) 'Paradoxical views on a paradoxical religion' in B. Boudewijnse, A.F. Droogers and F.H. Kamsteeg (eds.), *More than Opium: an Anthropological Approach to Latin American and Caribbean Pentecostal Praxis*, Lanham, Scarecrow, 1–34.

Edgell Becker, P. (1999) *Congregations in Conflict: Cultural Models of Local Religious Life*, New York and Cambridge, Cambridge University Press.

Eisenstadt, S. (1999) *Fundamentalism, Sectarianism and Revolutions: the Jacobin Dimension of Modernity*, Cambridge, Cambridge University Press.

(2000) 'Multiple Modernities', in *Daedalus*, 129/1: 1–30.

Elvy, P. (1986) *Buying Time: the Foundations of the Electronic Church*, Great Wakering, Essex, McCrimmons, for the Jerusalem Trust.

(1990) *The Future of Christian Broadcasting in Europe*, Great Wakering, Essex, McCrimmons, for the Jerusalem Trust.

Ester, P., Halman, L. and de Moor, R. (1994) *The Individualizing Society: Value Change in Europe and North America*, Tilburg, Tilburg University Press.

Fane, R. (1999) *A Religious Question for the 2001 Census*, unpublished M.Phil. thesis, University of Wales.

Finke, R. and Stark, R. (forthcoming) 'The dynamics of religious economies', in M. Dillon (ed.), *Handbook for the Sociology of Religion*, New York and Cambridge, Cambridge University Press.

Francis, L. (1997) 'The psychology of gender differences in religion: a review of empirical research', *Religion*, 27/1: 68–96.

Freston, P. (1996) 'The Protestant eruption into modern Brazilian politics', *Journal of Contemporary Religion*, 11/2: 147–68.

(1998a) 'Pentecostalism in Latin America: characteristics and controversies', *Social Compass*, 45/3: 335–58.

(1998b) 'Evangelicals and politics: a comparison between Africa and Latin America', *Journal of Contemporary Religion*, 13/2: 37–50.

(2001) *Evangelicals and Politics in Asia, Africa and Latin America*, Cambridge, Cambridge University Press.

Gerloff, R. (1992) *A Plea for Black African Theologies: the Black Church Movement in Britain in its Transatlantic Cultural and Theological Interaction*, Frankfurt, Peter Lang.

(2000) 'Editorial', *International Review of Mission*, 354: 275–80, special issue on the Cambridge Conference: a Milestone in Progress.

Gifford, P. (1992) *New Dimensions in African Christianity*, Nairobi, All Africa Conference of Churches.

(1995) *The Christian Churches and the Democratisation of Africa*, Leiden, Brill.

(1998) *African Christianity: its Public Role*, London, Hurst and Co.

Gill, A. (1998) *Rendering unto Caesar: the Roman Catholic Church and the State in Latin America*, Chicago, University of Chicago Press.

(1999) 'The struggle to be soul provider: Catholic responses to Protestant growth in Latin America', in C. Smith and J. Prokopy (eds.), *Latin American Religion in Motion*, New York, Routledge.

Göle, N. (2000) 'Snapshots of Islamic modernity', *Daedalus*, 129/1: 91–118.

Hackett, R. (1998) 'Charismatic/Pentecostal appropriation of media technologies in Nigeria and Ghana', *Journal of Religion in Africa*, XXVIII/3: 258–77.

Hadaway, K., Marler, P. and Chaves, M. (1993) 'What the polls don't show: a closer look at church attendance', *American Sociological Review*, 58/6: 741–52.

(1998) 'A symposium on church attendance', *American Sociological Review*, 63/1: 111–45.

Hadden, J. (1987) 'Religious broadcasting and the mobilization of the New Christian Right', *Journal for the Scientific Study of Religion*, 26/1: 1–24.

Hall, P. (1999) 'Social capital in Britain', *British Journal of Political Science*, 29/3: 417–62.

Halman, L. (2001) *The European Values Study: a Third Wave*, Tilburg, EVS, WORC, Tilburg University.

Halman, L. and Riis, O. (1999) *Religion in Secularizing Society, The European's Religion at the End of the 20th Century*, Tilburg, Tilburg University Press.

Harding, S., Phillips, D. with Fogarty, M. (1986) *Contrasting Values in Western Europe*, Basingstoke, Macmillan.

Hastings, A. (1994) *A History of African Christianity*, Oxford, Clarendon Press.

(2000) 'African Christian studies, 1967–1999: reflections of an editor', *Journal of Religion in Africa*, 30/1: 30–44.

Hervieu-Léger, D. (1999) *Le Pèlerin et le converti: la Religion en mouvement*, Paris, Flammarion.

(2000) *Religion as a Chain of Memory*, Cambridge, Polity Press.

Hong, Young-Gi (2000) 'Revisiting church growth: Korean Protestantism, a theological reflection', *International Review of Mission*, LXXXIX/353: 190–202.

Hoover, S. (1988) *Mass Media Religion: the Social Sources of the Electronic Church*, London, Sage.

(1998) *Religion in the News: Faith and Journalism in American Public Discourse*, London, Sage.

Horton, R. (1971) 'African Conversion', *Africa*, 41: 85–108.

Ileto, R.C. (1979) *Pasyon and Revolution: Popular Movements in the Philippines, 1840–1910*. Quezon City, Ateneo de Manila University Press.

Inglehart, R. (1997) *Modernization and Postmodernization: Cultural, Economic and Political Change in 43 Societies*, Princeton, Princeton University Press.

Inglehart, R. and Baker, W. (2000) 'Modernization, cultural change and the persistence of traditional values', *American Sociological Review*, 65/1: 19–51.

Ireland, R. (1991) *Kingdoms Come: Religion and Politics in Brazil*, Pittsburgh, PA, University of Pittsburgh Press.

Jenkins, T. (1999) *Religion in Everyday English Life; an Ethnographic Approach*, Oxford, Berghahn Books.

Kang, In-Chul (2000) 'Religion and the democratization movement', *Korea Journal*, 41/2: 224–47.

Kim, SungHo (2002) 'Rapid modernisation and the future of Korean Christianity', in *Religion*, 32/4.

Lalive D'Epinay, C. (1969) *Haven to the Masses: a Study of the Pentecostal Movement in Chile*, London, Lutterworth Press.

(1975) *Religion, dynamique sociale et dépendance: les mouvements protetants en Argentine et au Chili*, Paris and The Hague, Mouton.

Lehmann, D. (1990) *Democracy and Development in Latin America: Economics, Politics and Religion in the Postwar Period*, Cambridge, Polity Press.

(1996) *Struggle for the Spirit*, Cambridge, Polity Press.

Levine, D. (1995) 'Protestants and Catholics in Latin America: a family portrait', in M. Marty and S. Appleby (eds.), *Fundamentalisms Comprehended*, Chicago, University of Chicago Press, 155–78.

Levine, D. and Stoll, D. (1997) 'Bridging the gap between empowerment and power in Latin America', in S.H. Rudolph and J. Piscatori (eds.), *Transnational Religion and Fading States*, Boulder, CO, Westview, 63–103.

Lewis, B. and Schnapper, D. (1994) (eds.) *Muslims and Europe*, London, Pinter.

Lienesch, M. (1993) *Redeeming America: Piety and Politics in the New Christian Right*, Chapel Hill, University of North Carolina Press.

Lipset, S. (1996) *American Exceptionalism: a Double-Edged Sword*, New York, Norton.

Livesey, L. (2000) (ed.) *Public Religion and Urban Transformation: Faith in the City*, New York, New York University Press.

Longley, C. (1991) *The Times Book of Clifford Longley*, London, HarperCollins.

Löwy, M. (2001) 'Rapports entre le religieux et le politique en Amérique latine', *Archives de Sciences Sociales des Religions*, 114: 61–6.

Luca, N. (2000) 'La conquête de la modernité par les nouveaux mouvements chrétiens coréens', *Social Compass*, 525–40.

List of References   173

Lynas, S. (2001) *The Churches' Experience of the Millennium*, London, Churches Together in England.

Lyon, D. and Van Die, M. (2000) (eds.) *Rethinking Church, State and Modernity: Canada between Europe and the USA*, Toronto, University of Toronto Press.

Maggay, M. (1998) 'Towards sensitive engagement with Filipino indigenous consciousness', *International Review of Mission*, LXXXVII/346: 361–73.

Maldonado, J. (1993) 'Building "fundamentalism" from the family in Latin America', in M. Marty and S. Appleby (eds.), *Fundamentalisms and Society*, Chicago, University of Chicago Press, 214–39.

Mariz, C. (1990) 'Ingrejas pentecostais e estratégias de sobreviviência', in J. Braga (ed.), *Religião e cidadania*, Bahia, DEA-UFBA-EGBA, 89–112.

— (1994) *Coping with Poverty: Pentecostals and Christian Base Communities in Brazil*, Philadelphia, Temple University Press.

Marshall-Fratani, R. (1998) 'Mediating the global and the local in Nigerian Pentecostalism', *Journal of Religion in Africa*, XXVIII/3: 278–315.

Martin, B. (2001) 'The Pentecostal gender paradox' in R. Fenn (ed.), *The Blackwell Companion to the Sociology of Religion*, Oxford, Blackwell, 52–66.

Martin, D. (1978) *A General Theory of Secularization*, Oxford, Blackwell.

— (1990) *Tongues of Fire: the Explosion of Protestantism in Latin America*, Oxford, Blackwell.

— (1991) 'The secularization issue: prospect and retrospect', *British Journal of Sociology*, 42/4: 466–74.

— (1996a) *Forbidden Revolutions*, London, SPCK.

— (1996b) 'Remise en question de la théorie de la sécularisation', in G. Davie and D. Hervieu-Léger (eds.), *Identités religieuses en Europe*. Paris, La Découverte, 25–42.

— (2001a) *Pentecostalism: the World their Parish*, Oxford, Blackwell.

— (2001b) 'Personal Reflections in the Mirror of Halévy and Weber', in R. Fenn (ed.), *The Blackwell Companion to the Sociology of Religion*, Oxford, Blackwell, 23–38.

Marty, M. and Appleby, S. (1995) (eds.) *Fundamentalisms Comprehended*, Chicago, Chicago University Press.

Maxwell, D. (1998) ' "Delivered from the spirit of poverty?" Pentecostalism, prosperity and modernity in Zimbabwe', *Journal of Religion in Africa*, XXVIII/3: 350–73.

— (1999) *Christians and Chiefs in Zimbabwe*, Edinburgh, Edinburgh University Press.

— (2001) 'Introduction', in D. Maxwell with I. Lawrie (eds.), *Christianity and the African Imagination: Essays in Honour of Adrian Hastings*, Leiden, Brill.

Medhurst, K. (2000) 'Christianity and the Future of Europe', in M. Percy (ed.), *Calling Time: Religion and Change at the Turn of the Millennium*, Sheffield, Sheffield Academic Press, 143–62.

Meyer, B. (1998) ' "Make a complete break with the past". Memory and post-colonial modernity in Ghanaian Pentecostal discourse', in *Journal of Religion in Africa*, XXVIII/3: 316–49.

— (1999) *Translating the Devil: Religion and Modernity among the Ewe in Ghana*, Edinburgh, Edinburgh University Press.

Miguez, D. (1998) *Spiritual Bonfire in Argentina*, Amsterdam, CEDLA.

Miranda-Feliciano, F. (1991) 'Renewal movements and evangelism', *International Review of Mission*, LXXX/317: 61–70.

Muller, S. (1997) 'Time to kill: Europe and the politics of leisure', *The National Interest*, 48: 26–36.

Nielsen, J. (1995) *Muslims and Western Europe*, Edinburgh, Edinburgh University Press.

Noll, M. (2000) *American Evangelical Christianity: an Introduction*, Oxford, Blackwell.

O'Connell, J. (1991) *The Making of Modern Europe: Strengths, Constraints and Resolutions* (University of Bradford, Peace Research Report, no. 26).

O'Toole, R. (1996) 'Religion in Canada: its development and contemporary situation', *Social Compass*, 43/1: 119–34.

Pace, E. and Guolo, R. (1998) *Il Fondamentalismo*, Roma-Bari, Editori Laterza.

Park, Seong-Won (1997) 'A survey on mission work in the Korean churches', *International Review of Mission*, XXXVI/342: 329–44.

Park, Yong-Shin (2000) 'Protestant Christianity and its place in changing Korea', in *Social Compass*, 47/4: 507–25.

Peck, J. (1993) *The Gods of Televangelism: the Crisis of Meaning and the Appeal of Religious Televangelism*, Creskill, NJ, Hampton Press.

Peel, J. (2000) *Religious Encounter and the Making of the Yoruba*, Bloomington, IN, Indiana University Press.

Putnam, R. (1995) 'Bowling alone: America's declining social capital', *Journal of Democracy*, 6: 65–78.

(2000) *Bowling Alone: the Collapse and Revival of American Community*, New York, Simon and Schuster.

Putnam, R. with Leonardi, R. and Nanetti, R. (1993) *Making Democracy Work: Civil Traditions in Modern Italy*, Princeton, Princeton University Press

Quicke, A., and Quicke, J. (1992) *Hidden Agendas: The Politics of Religious Broadcasting in Britain, 1987–91*, Virginia Beach, VA, Dominion Kings Grant Publications.

Ranger, T. (2000) Review of B. Sundkler and C. Steed, *A History of the Church in Africa*, Cambridge, Cambridge University Press, in *Journal of Religion in Africa*, XXX/4: 482–6.

Robbers, G. (1996) (ed.) *Church and State in the European Union*, Baden-Baden, Nomos Verlagsgesellschaft.

Roof, W.C. (1993) *A Generation of Seekers*, San Francisco, Harper San Francisco.

(1999) *Spiritual Marketplace, Baby Boomers and the Remaking of American Religion*, Princeton, Princeton University Press.

(2000) 'Spiritual seeking in the United States: report of a panel study', *Archives de Sciences Sociales des Religions*, 109: 49–66.

Rose, S. (1996) 'The politics of Philippine fundamentalism', in D. Westerlund (ed.), *Questioning the Secular State: the Worldwide Resurgence of Religion in Politics*, London, Hurst and Co., 323–55.

Runciman, W. (1983/1988) *A Treatise on Social Theory*, Cambridge, Cambridge University Press (2 volumes).

List of References 175

Schmied, G. (1996) 'American Televangelism in German TV', *Journal of Contemporary Religion*, 11/1: 95–9.

Simpson, J. (1990) 'The Stark-Bainbridge theory of religion', *Journal for the Scientific Study of Religion*, 29/3: 367–71.

—— (2000) 'Religion and politics in post-industrial democratic societies', paper presented to the BSA Sociology of Religion Study Group Conference, Exeter (April 2000).

Skog, M. (2001) Religion in Sweden, unpublished paper.

Smith, C. (1998) *American Evangelicalism: Embattled and Thriving*, Chicago, Chicago University Press.

Smith, S. and Prokopy, J. (1999) (eds.) *Latin American Religion in Motion*, New York, Routledge.

Social Indicators in Korea (1999) Seoul, National Statistical Office of the Republic of Korea.

Stark, R. and Bainbridge, W. (1985) *The Future of Religion*, Berkeley, University of California Press.

—— (1987) *A Theory of Religion*, New York, Peter Lang.

Stoetzel, J. (1983) *Les Valeurs du temps présent*, Paris, Presses Universitaires de France.

Sundkler, B. (1948) *Bantu Prophets of South Africa*, London, Lutterworth Press.

Sundkler, B. and Steed, C. (2000) *A History of the Church in Africa*, Cambridge, Cambridge University Press.

Ter Haar, G. (1998a) 'African Christianity in The Netherlands', in G. Ter Haar (ed.), *Strangers and Sojourners: Religious Communities in the Diaspora*, Leuven, Peeters.

—— (1998b) *Halfway to Paradise*, Cardiff, Cardiff Academic Press.

Timms, N. (1992) *Family and Citizenship: Values in Contemporary Britain*, Aldershot, Dartmouth.

Turner, H. (1977) *Bibliography of New Religious Movements in Primal Societies: Black Africa*, Boston, G.K. Hall.

Vertovec, S. and Peach, C. (1997) (eds.) *Islam in Europe. The Politics of Religion and Community*, Basingstoke, Macmillan and Warwick, CRER.

Walls, A. (1996) 'Introduction: African Christianity in the History of Religions' in C. Fyfe and A. Walls (eds.), *Christianity in Africa in the 1990s*, Edinburgh, Centre of African Studies.

Walter, A. J. and Davie, G. (1998) 'The religiosity of women in the modern West', *British Journal of Sociology*, 49/4: 640–60.

Ward, K. (1999) 'Africa', in A. Hastings (ed.), *A World History of Christianity*, London, Cassell.

Warner, S. (1993) 'Work in progress towards a new paradigm for the sociological study of religion in the United States', *American Journal of Sociology*, 98/5: 1044–93

—— (1997) 'A paradigm is not a theory: reply to Lechner', *American Journal of Sociology*, 103/1: 192–8.

Warner, S. and Wittner, J. (1998) (eds.) *Gatherings in Diaspora: Religious Communities and the New Immigration*, Philadelphia, Temple University Press.

Wasserstein, B. (1996) *Vanishing Diaspora. The Jews in Europe since 1945*, London, Hamish Hamilton.

Webber, J. (1994) (ed.) *Jewish Identities in the New Europe*, London, Washington, Littman Library of Jewish Civilization.

Weiming, Tu (1996) 'The quest for meaning: religion in the People's Republic of China', in P. Berger (ed.), *The Desecularization of the World: Resurgent Religion and World Politics*, Grand Rapids, Eerdmans Publishing Co.

Willems, E. (1954) 'Protestantism as a factor of cultural change in Brazil', *Economic Development and Cultural Change*, 3: 321–33.

(1964) 'Protestantism and culture change in Brazil', in E. Baklanoff (ed.), *New Perspective of Brazil*, Nashville, Vanderbilt University.

(1967) *Followers of the New Faith: Culture Change and the Rise of Protestantism in Brazil and Chile*, Nashville, TN, Vanderbilt University Press.

Wilson, B. (1982) *Religion in Sociological Perspective*, Oxford, Oxford University Press.

Woodhead, L. (2002) 'Religion and Gender', in L. Woodhead, P. Fletcher, H. Kawanani and D. Smith, (eds.), *Religions in the Modern World: Traditions and Transformations*, London, Routledge, 323–56.

Wuthnow, R. (1999) *After Heaven: Spirituality in America since the 1950s*, Princeton, Princeton University Press.

Yearbook of Korean Religion (1993), edited by the Korea Research Institute for Religion and Society, Seoul, Halimwon.

Yoon, Yee-Heum (1997) 'The contemporary religious situation in Korea, in L. Lancaster and R. Payne (eds.), *Religion and Society in Contemporary Korea*, Berkeley, Institute of East Asian Studies, University of California, 1–18.

Young, L. (1997) *Rational Choice Theory and Religion: Summary and Assessment*, New York and London, Routledge.

INDEX

Park, Y. 133, 134
Parsons, T. 14
Patterson, Bishop 135
Peel, J. 94–5, 102
Pentecostals 17, 22–3, 25, 54–83,
    84, 99–102, 105–7, 109–10,
    112, 116, 121, 131, 139–40,
    144–5, 151, 159
Pereira Leite, P. 81
Philippine Episcopal Church 116
pluralism 15–16, 39, 53, 57, 72,
    112
Pope 22, 114–15
possession cults *see* spiritists
Putnam, R. 35–6, 47

Rastafarians 106, 108
rational choice theory (RCT) 15,
    41–5, 50, 77–8, 151
Robbers, G. 12
Rose, S. 123
Rousseau, J.-J. 37
Runciman, W. 27, 145

Sabbatarians 108
Santeria 106
secularisation thesis 13–16, 20,
    24, 41, 43, 58, 75–7, 95,
    120–1, 123, 142, 146–7, 150–2,
    156, 159, 161
Sephardim 9
shamanism 124

Shembe, I. 96
Sikhs 10, 51
spiritists 59, 63, 74, 81
Stark, R. 42, 78
Steed, C. 86, 91
Stoll, D. 71
Sundkler, B. 86, 91–4, 97
syncretism 57, 72, 106

televangelism 32, 61–2
Ter Haar, G. 85, 108–10
Tincq, H. 48
Turner, H. 98

Umbanda 57, 74, 105–6
United Churches 53

vicarious religion 19–20, 44, 76
voluntarism 18, 35–6, 52, 54, 73,
    82, 149
Voodoo 106

Walls, A. 87, 89–90
Warner, S. 43
Weber, M. 19, 25, 64, 70, 157
Willems, E. 64
Wilson, B. 14, 16, 74

Young, L. 42

Zimbabwe Assemblies of God,
    Africa (ZAOGA) 101
Zion Christian Church 96